FLYING HIGH

Flying High

Remembering Barry Goldwater

WILLIAM F. BUCKLEY JR.

A Member of the Perseus Books Group
New York

Books published by Basic Books are available at special
discounts for bulk purchases in the United States by
corporations, institutions, and other organizations. For
more information, please contact the Special Markets
Department at the Perseus Books Group, 2300 Chestnut
Street, Suite 200, Philadelphia, PA 19103, or call (800)
255-1514, or e-mail special.markets@perseusbooks.com.

Designed by Brent Wilcox

Library of Congress Cataloging-in-Publication Data
Buckley, William F. (William Frank), 1925–
  Flying high : remembering Barry Goldwater /
William F. Buckley, Jr.
     p.   cm.
  Includes index.
  ISBN-13: 978-0-465-00836-0 (alk. paper)
  ISBN-10: 0-465-00836-4 (alk. paper)
    1. Goldwater, Barry M. (Barry Morris), 1909–1998.
  2. Goldwater, Barry M. (Barry Morris), 1909–1998—
Friends and associates.   3. Conservatism—United
States—History—20th century.   4. Presidential
candidates—United States—Biography.   5. United
States—Politics and government—1945–1989.
  6. Legislators—United States—Biography.   7. United
States. Congress. Senate—Biography.   8. Buckley,
William F. (William Frank), 1925–   9. Young
Americans for Freedom.   I. Title.
  E748.G64B83 2008
  973.92092—dc22
  [B]
                                        2007036392

10 9 8 7 6 5 4 3 2

For Evan G. Galbraith, with affection

CONTENTS

CONTENTS

INTRODUCTION

This slim volume tells a story. The storyteller is the author. No attempt is made to conceal this, and if the story were comprehensively retold, the author's role would probably be more conspicuous, not less so.

I am the founder of a conservative journal which took its place, very soon after its nativity, at the center of conservative political analysis in America. I, and others, expressed our resolve to resist collectivist solutions to problems at home and unprofitable accommodationism in foreign policy. Insights and formulations about which we felt strongly were being ignored by others on the political scene—at times suppressed, at times awkwardly misrepresented. What we did about it is the subject of this book.

We needed, for instance, a youth movement, and so we founded Young Americans for Freedom. We needed a national political figure around whom to consolidate, and so we transfigured Barry Goldwater. We needed to stimulate resistance to the endemic wiles of the Soviet bid for the world, and so we trained our eyes on what the Soviet legions were up to and on the movements of their central figures, especially Nikita Khrushchev, looking in on him moment by moment when he visited the United States.

We were all over the place and accordingly Flying High. At the same time we were earthily present in nooks and crannies of political and intellectual life in the two decades when all of this happened.

What was it like to edit *National Review*? We take the reader to an editorial conference with the magazine's early architects, men and women of disparate inclinations and strengths. One of them is commissioned to ghostwrite a little book for Barry Goldwater expressing "Americanist" views, and seven months later he turns in the manuscript of *The Conscience of a Conservative*. It is an overwhelming success, and it shapes the thinking of the Republican Party, which nominates the author—Goldwater—for the presidency.

This book recalls the many distractions that arose in the attempt to formulate wise and attractive positions for Goldwater as political candidate. And it revisits a private meeting at Palm Beach at which five people, including Goldwater, express themselves on such problems as the John Birch Society, which sought, with the best of intentions, to arrest productive right-wing thinking, substituting for it the hypothesis that our leaders were Communist dupes. This was here and there seriously contended, and some conservatives were seduced by the argument.

Senator Goldwater ultimately chose, in his campaign for president, to follow the advice of two or three men whose hold on politics was insecure. He knew all along that the fight to depose President Lyndon Johnson was political romance, but he gave in to the draft-Goldwater surge in order to infuse his party with a human and humane liveliness that would endure long after his defeat, awaiting formal validation with Ronald Reagan.

Reagan is not a major figure in *Flying High*, although we were very good friends and he was a faithful and outspoken partisan of *National Review*. I do touch on his contributions to the Goldwater campaign, especially the famous televised speech. But it seemed right to linger in this reminiscence at the side of Barry Goldwater as he pilots his plane down to Phoenix, the evening lights just coming on. There he would suffer the great political humiliation just ahead. It was assumed that his brand of thought would lie buried forever in the ash heap of American politics, but it would prove not to be so. One year later he would among other things be visiting *National Review* in New York, and enlivening those— among them the author of this very personal reminiscence— who had been standing by, doing our own things.

The reader is entitled to ask if the material here is factually reliable. *Reliable* is the perfect word in this context. The book is not strictly factual, in that conversations are reported which cannot be documented as having taken place word for word. Yet it is reliable in that these words might well have been spoken. There are zero distortions here—no thought is engrafted in anyone that alters the subject's character, or inclinations, or even habits of speech. If General Eisenhower can't be proved by divine auditors to have spoken the words here placed in his mouth, it is as certain as the ears on the reader's head that such words were substantially those that were spoken, depicting Eisenhower's thoughts and expressions. There are one or two scenes which, though entirely congruent with what happened, are entirely fictitious, e.g., the description of the young aide on the airplane carrying Henry Cabot Lodge and Nikita Khrushchev to California. Such are there to enliven, and to be enjoyed.

It was a grand time we had, providing all that political experiences could yield, joys and sorrows, excitement and depression. It would have been wrong, and ungrateful, to keep all of this to oneself.

Prologue

B arry Goldwater traveled everywhere, and one time we found ourselves together in a remote place. I was less surprised to see the 1964 Republican candidate for president in Christchurch, New Zealand, eight years after his presidential campaign, than he was to see me. Barry Goldwater was a hardy naturalist, son of the sun of Arizona deserts, and a man of exploration and science. No tool of the trade, in his fields of interest, was unfamiliar to him, and none failed to attract his attention. The airplane was in his blood, and the radio, and instruments of magnification and miniaturization. He was perpetually curious about oddities of nature and geography, and he always had at hand the most alluring paraphernalia, cameras especially. Although I had flown in his airplane with him, pirouetting about the Grand Canyon, he teased me now, bound for the Antarctic, that my interest in natural wonders was synthetic—that I was drawn to other adornments of life. When, many years later, I performed a harpsichord concerto in Phoenix, a reporter accosted him, asking how, in the senator's judgment, Mr. Buckley had acquitted himself. Goldwater replied, "Wonderfully. Absolutely first rate." He paused. "Of course, this is the first time I ever went to a concert."

Neither of us had known the other was on the roster of this trip. There were a dozen of us altogether, the latest crew of a regular pilgrimage brought together by the Secretary of the Navy every other year to publicize the American enterprise in the Antarctic. Our country's role began as a celebration of the International Geophysical Year in 1957, a common undertaking of a dozen nations, featuring the United States and the Soviet Union. The principals had made an enduring commitment to maintain two stations in the Antarctic: one of them housing at least twelve American scientists and a single Soviet scientist, the second housing at least twelve Soviets and a single American. The alien scientist had a symbolic role, a reminder that the geophysical expeditions were nonpartisan. And, we all assumed, the extranational scientist also served a peekaboo purpose, to assure that neither monolith was turning its Antarctic igloo into a laboratory for the development of ice-age warfare.

Goldwater, child of the Grand Canyon, was always impressed by sheer magnitude, and the dimensions we would be visiting were very grand indeed. Antarctica is larger than the United States and Mexico combined. Its coastline is eleven thousand miles long. During the winter, the ice doubles the size of the continent. The ice at the South Pole is about two miles thick. If it were all to melt, the water level of the world would rise by two hundred feet, which means that the first fourteen stories of the Empire State Building would be under water. The ice in Antarctica is a deposit of 90 percent of the earth's supply of fresh water.

Goldwater pulled out, from a deep pocket of the heavy GI trousers we had all been issued, a sheet of figures. Ocean water absorbs 90 percent of the sun's heat. Snow and ice reflect 85 percent. Secretary of the Navy John Chafee, our host, had supplied Goldwater with a few graphic words. "This tells you," Goldwater held the paper up to the light, "that Antarctica is the principal generator of the energy that governs the metabolism of the earth. Its effect on weather currents and temperature is critical. Its potential uses, if we"—he pointed his finger at his throat—"us and our Russian pals out there—if we come to know how to domesticate Antarctica, that would be, Chafee's memo said, something very like the development of a key"—he simulated a key in hand, turning his wrist—"a key to the universe. Satisfied, Buckley?"

I admitted my derelict ignorance of these universes.

"Okay, just take it from me. There is everything there, potentially: the control of the weather; the answer to the fresh-water problem. A vat of energy greater than the known supply of the world's oil. If I had been elected president, you'd have seen it all come to life." Goldwater pursed his lips into that muted, mischievous smile, as he had so many times done over a lifetime in politics. He had the ability to attract a kind of devotional concern, the very same that had animated a majority of the delegates at the 1964 convention in San Francisco, who had made him their presidential candidate.

We had ahead of us a hideous eight-hour plane ride, lying on our backs, maneuvering for comfort by twisting ourselves about with our legs splayed out. It was a naval transport, a C–130 "Herc" turboprop. Secretary Chafee was humiliated at having to use it, but no jet plane could be trusted to land at our destination. Although it was summertime in Antarctica, the runway was unreliably icy. The airplane would deposit us at the thousand-man U.S. naval base at McMurdo, from which we would set out the next day on an eight-hundred-mile journey in a small plane with ski-like landing gear. On consecutive days we would undertake our formal visits to the tiny scientific quarries. In 1957, Moscow had coveted the post at the actual South Pole, and so had we. We won the coin toss; the Soviet Union got the magnetic South Pole, seven hundred miles distant. In these little outposts the two teams of scientists labored with their instruments, periodically receiving supplies by airplane. In the winter months the airplanes can't land but have to drop their supplies. Neither site receives a human visitor in those months.

At McMurdo I suggested to Goldwater that we team up with his son Barry Jr., Member of Congress, and my brother Jim, United States Senator, who were also members of the delegation. I suggested a drink at the McMurdo Station BOQ, but Goldwater communicated the grave news that he was on the wagon for a month. We attempted festiveness nonetheless, and chatted with brother Jim and son Barry, and with our host, Secretary Chafee, about the exciting time ahead.

Two days later, at noontime, I was sitting in the crowded Soviet igloo at the magnetic South Pole. At my side were Barry Jr. and one Vostov, a talkative Russian scientist who knew no English. From time to time he would reach out over the crowded floor-level dining canvas we ate from, seeking help from an interpreter. Every five minutes he would pass great trays of caviar and tumblers of vodka, the sounds of amity welling from our cramped bodies as we ate and drank and ignored the Cold War. I acknowledged and returned a Russian toast to peace and prosperity, and then broke to respond to Barry Jr.'s sharp elbow thrust—"*My dad wants to see you*," he whispered to me, pointing to the igloo's entrance. Senator Goldwater, peering in from the dark cold, motioned me to follow him. I worked my way up and out, and followed him into the adjoining igloo. We ducked in quickly, dodging the outside temperature of 56 degrees below zero.

"Thought you might like to talk to your wife," he grinned, disguising the pride he felt at having maneuvered the Soviet radio to contrive a quick conversation with his own wife in sunny Phoenix. I was speechless as he handed me the receiver. In a few moments I heard the telephone ringing. After an interval, my wife's voice.

"It's me, darling," I said rapturously.

There was a pause. "Do you realize what time it is? It's three o'clock in the morning!"

"I'm calling from the South Pole!"

"Oh. Well, hello."

That was all the air time we had. I turned to see, standing by, my Russian buddy, Vostov. He somehow communicated that he had a special gift for me. At lunch he had pleaded with me to give him U.S. bills of whatever denomination. I fished out and gave him everything I had, which amounted to fifteen dollars. His elation was all-consuming.

Now, outside the radio room, he was bent on reciprocity. He thrust a ten-pound cardboard packet into my arms. "It's for you!"

The interpreter explained, "Vostov says this is a block of ice he pulled up this morning. It was formed 25,000 years ago and has been frozen ever since."

I carried the block on my lap on the ninety-minute flight back from the Russian outpost. Reaching McMurdo, I got from the naval sick bay twelve urine-specimen bottles, and poured into them the melted remains of my precious ice, most of which had drizzled away in transit. When I reached home with my bottle collection, I made up labels recounting the contents' history, and sent each of my South Pole companions a souvenir bottle, properly labeled. Ten years later, when I was visiting Goldwater at his house, he dug up the keepsake and showed it to me. About half of the 25,000-year-old water had evaporated.

Returning to Christchurch, Goldwater was bound for home, I for Hawaii, as had been scheduled before the South Pole came into sight. There I would join up with fellow journalists who had been selected to accompany President Richard Nixon on his celebrated opening to China. It was rather a sad parting, back at Christchurch. Barry and I swore we would never, ever travel again to Antarctica, except in company with each other.

1

Stirrings in Chicago

The Republican convention of 1960 was a political watershed. Dwight Eisenhower attended it, in the eighth and concluding year of his presidency. He was the grand old man on the political scene, though not exciting to anyone except his biographers and veterans of D-Day. He was widely thought of as "conservative." He liked it that way and from time to time reinforced this perception by re-designating himself as such.

On the matter of his political eminence, there was no question. Ike could be thought of as simply owning the Chicago convention. Yet there were reservations about his leadership, though mostly expressed, if at all, cautiously. And it was certainly true of the majority of the delegates that they thought of Eisenhower as a leader who was substantially spent, and, more, a leader who had neglected several opportunities to cement his identification with the right wing.

There had been, to begin with, the divisive McCarthy business.

Senator Joe McCarthy, most of his supporters would have agreed, went too far and became irredeemably sloppy. Still, they thought of him as the political embodiment of the anti-Communist cause. By December 1954, Joe McCarthy's mistakes had proved fatal. He had alienated the majority of his colleagues in the Senate, including one-half of his fellow Republicans.

What happened to McCarthy was historically extraordinary. The vote to censure him was affirmed by all the Democratic senators—and half the sitting Republicans (not including Goldwater, then in his first term). This was only the fourth censure of the century.

His colleagues might as well have voted to vaporize him. From appearing almost every day on the front pages of the nation's newspapers (dating back to the famous speech in 1950 in which he had charged the State Department with tolerating Communists on its payroll), he all but disappeared. Diligent inquirers would learn that what he mostly did after the censure (and, substantially, in the months before the censure) was drink—drink to devastating excess. He was not a falling-down drunk, but he essentially abandoned the causes he had associated himself with. He paid only formal attention to Senate proceedings.

Even so, when, two and a half years after the censure, he died, the funeral he was given was the splashiest farewell since FDR's. By 1960, three years after McCarthy's death, many Republicans still resented, or were saddened by, President Eisenhower's vocal opposition to McCarthy in the critical years. By that time, most conservatives were prepared to forget the senator's inglorious exaggerations. They liked simply to celebrate the memory of him as the champion anti-Communist, defiant of the accommodationist majority, which was prepared to accept permanently the division of the planet with the Communist empire.

As a candidate for president in 1952, Eisenhower had called attention to the perils of interventionist government and to the dangers of inflation, and he had inveighed against the welfare state. Even then, he didn't share the views of some Republican conservatives. Candidate Eisenhower criticized the big-government programs of Truman's Fair Deal, but Old Guard Republicans talked about eliminating not just the Fair Deal of President Truman, but also the New Deal of FDR. In any case, once he became president, Eisenhower had called for a moderate Republicanism which would preserve individual freedom and the market economy but also ensure assistance to jobless workers and to non-affluent senior citizens. He intended, he said, to lead the country "down the middle of the road between the unfettered power of concentrated wealth ... and the unbridled power of statism or partisan interests."

He went on to sign legislation to expand Social Security and to increase the minimum wage. He created a Department of Health, Education, and Welfare and extended government aid for low-income housing. His most ambitious domestic project, the Interstate Highway program, created a 41,000-mile road system. This project, the President was proud to note, involved enough concrete to build "six side-walks to the moon." All very well, some of the old-timers complained, but what's the matter with letting the states undertake these improvements on the infrastructure?

Eisenhower did use his veto to block some expensive Democratic programs, but critics called attention to the figures. In 1953, domestic spending had been 31 percent of the federal budget. Seven years later, it had risen to 49 percent.

The majority of the delegates at the 1960 Republican convention in Chicago were prepared to celebrate Dwight Eisenhower as a great national figure. But, as noted, most were also glad that he was moving on. The 22nd Amendment to the Constitution, deemed by some a retroactive gesture of spite against Franklin Delano Roosevelt, forbade a third presidential term. In private conversation Eisenhower had berated that amendment as anti-democratic, contradicting what might be a public demand for more from the same leader (he had himself in mind). But the convention delegates in 1960 would not have nominated Ike for a third term and were relieved that the Constitution forbade them even to consider the question.

The mood in Chicago, therefore, was that of a constituency wanting more, but not exactly more of the same. Everyone knew that the delegates would have to vote for Vice President Richard Nixon, and his past was reassuring to many who thought Ike too much the appeaser, at home and abroad. Nixon's independent political reputation traced back to his championing, in 1948, of Whittaker Chambers in the great, melodramatic showdown against Alger Hiss. Hiss's supporters could not have known, in 1948, how slavishly he had served as a Communist agent. Many, unaware of his Soviet ties, were prepared to support him simply as the victim of anti-Communist fundamentalism.

So Chambers counted in Nixon's favor in Chicago, as did the invigorating partisanship he almost always generated. Second only to McCarthy himself, Nixon was the sacred enemy of the American left wing, which made him something of a venerated figure among Republican activists— many of them convention delegates.

But for not a few Republicans, especially younger ones, there was something unsatisfactory even about Nixon. He himself had an accommodationist streak, demonstrated by his constant excuse-making for every error in judgment that Eisenhower ever made. So while he would be affirmed as the successor designate, he did not stir the convention, even as, three months later, he would not stir the American people, who passed the presidency on to John F. Kennedy.

But Vice President Nixon had the grit and skill of a seasoned politician. He had been busy in the weeks and months before the convention, courting delegates and propitiating their concerns. When the moment came to vote, there was no other figure on the scene prepared to be in serious competition for the nomination. But there was such a figure in the shadows. The little congregation that met at the Buckley family home in Sharon, Connecticut, in August, a week after the GOP convention, knew this, or sensed it. But we would have a detailed report from Marvin Liebman, roving ambassador of the American right wing, and everybody's best friend.

Marvin was well situated to report on what had happened at Chicago because he had been there, exchanging opinions with every figure in conservative America. Marvin was an ingratiating independent operator. A decade earlier he had been a young fighting partisan in defense of the young state of Israel, and a member of the Communist Party.

Like so many in the activist political world exposed to the ugliness of the Communist faith, he went from full-time member of the movement to full-time opponent. Liebman now associated himself with almost any private organization engaged in opposition to Communist activity, whether in the Soviet Union, or China, or Eastern Europe, Korea, Indochina, Greece, Africa. Rick Perlstein, in his colorful book on Goldwater, *Before the Storm*, wrote of Liebman that he was "the maestro of the bipartisan committees, the testimonial dinners, the rallies, the full-page ads, the crowded letters with the preprinted signatures for committees with long names. His masterpiece was the Committee of One Million, which had supposedly collected a million signatures to keep Red China out of the United Nations."

Marvin Liebman was a close personal and professional friend of the Buckleys. This meant me, the founder and editor of *National Review*; my wife, Patricia; and various siblings, especially Priscilla, managing editor of *NR*; Patricia (and her husband, Brent Bozell); James, a future U.S. senator; and Maureen and Jane, associate editors at *NR*.

Marvin, sentimental and loyal, was adept at seeing humor in almost any situation, and at prolonging it. He reported—Marvin was taking cocktails in Sharon with several of the Buckleys—that, at the convention, denunciations of Mao Tse-tung hadn't been as declamatory as he would have liked. One motion, threatening withdrawal from the United Nations if it admitted Red China, didn't get off the floor— "We got only thirty or forty delegates."

Still, Marvin had gotten earthy satisfaction from the Chicago scene. Lame duck Dwight Eisenhower was soaringly present in his final address as president. Vice President Richard Nixon, undeviating from his plan to achieve the nomination for president, had been relieved when his only viable competitor, Nelson Rockefeller, governor of New York, had withdrawn from the race. But Rockefeller would remain a strategic armed political encampment Nixon would need always to cope with. Henry Cabot Lodge was there in Chicago. He had lost his Senate seat in a squeaker to the young John F. Kennedy in 1952 and then saved face by accepting Eisenhower's appointment as ambassador to the United Nations. In Chicago, Nixon secured his political flank among moderates by naming Lodge his running mate.

"Lodge is okay," Marvin told us. To the *National Review* crowd, that meant that he would take the anti-Communist side, and would accept the post-Eisenhower designation of the GOP as a conservative political party. "But of course," Marvin continued, "Lodge doesn't have the firepower of Walter Judd." Judd was a compendium of Republican conservative virtues. He had worked as a medical doctor and as a missionary in China; he was a longtime member of Congress; he was keynote speaker at this convention—and he was a founder of the Committee of One Million.

Through it all, Marvin advised his friends in Sharon, there was one magical figure. That figure, he said, on whom the hopes of the American Right were slowly crystallizing in Chicago, was United States Senator Barry Goldwater.

Goldwater wasn't a candidate in 1960, yet he had arrived as a political figure of singular eminence. Within three days, said Marvin, Goldwater had become the emotional idol of the majority of the delegates. "They weren't ready to bring on a political cataclysm by ditching Nixon and nominating Barry for president, but they'd have elected him king." All he had to do, said Liebman with great solemnity, was disclose that his blood was truly blue, never mind his frontier mother and Jewish merchant father and Arizona-sand-and-sunshine complexion. Besides, and above all, Goldwater was the author of *The Conscience of a Conservative*.

Need one say more? That slim little book of political and moral commandments told it all, Marvin reminded his friends. And most of the delegates in Chicago were aware of it. "It's amazing to remember, but that book was first published by a vanity house."

"Yes," Brent Bozell nodded, quickly adding, "but that whole operation was carried forward under the tireless patronage of Clarence Manion." Manion was a leading figure in the conservative movement. He had been dean of the law school at Notre Dame, had been appointed by President Eisenhower to a presidential commission, and was an author and radio broadcaster.

"Right, Brent, right," Marvin was professionally deferential. "And you actually wrote that book, and not only that, you spent three months promoting it!"

Brent shrugged modestly and shifted in his seat, saying nothing.

But Marvin was already going on. "And who could have predicted—a publishing and political sensation!"

That was no exaggeration. Its beginning, in April 1960, had been modest—with an initial press run of five thousand—but by the time the convention met in Chicago, it was selling by the tens of thousands and being hailed as a lighthouse of libertarian thought. It was even likened, by its special fans, to Thomas Paine's *Common Sense*.

Goldwater had brought a supernal charm and utterly American savoir-faire into twentieth-century politics at a time when U.S. policy had become a gymnast's complex of special interests, international entanglements, and straitening legislation. To his scattered supporters, he offered hope of cutting through all of this. "I would rather see the Republicans lose in 1960 fighting on principle," he proclaimed, "than I would care to see us win standing on grounds we know are wrong and on which we will ultimately destroy ourselves."

In Chicago there was this phenomenon: serious, avid, bright young people with stars in their eyes, but not led by the bookish abstractions of ideological nostrums. These young people ("two or three hundred," Marvin guessed), were of a recognizable breed—"like the kids on the other side who plead for conferences with the Soviet Union and for an end to nuclear armament and the military-industrial complex. But they aren't," Marvin went on, "like the young Jewish intellectuals attracted to Henry Wallace in the forties. These kids—grown kids; they're in their late teens and twenties—have names like Adams and Baker and . . . and . . . "

"Carlisle?" I volunteered.

"Yeah," Marvin laughed. "They're politically minded, some of them active in state and national organizations upholding loyalty oaths, campaigning for the right to work without joining a union, supporting investigating committees in the tradition of Senator McCarthy.

"What's special about them," Marvin continued, "is how they feel the call of a mission where Communism is concerned." His eyes twinkled. "American counterparts of the pro-Communist activists whose efforts they want to frustrate."

Those of us gathered that evening in Sharon, middle-aged, recently young, listened with a shared involvement. We had seen Marvin in action over several years, and we weren't surprised that he had become a kind of father figure to the young right-wing Republicans. Though himself a tee-totaler, he would stay up late hours with the activists, in hotel suites, meeting rooms, bars, as they lamented Richard Nixon's capitulation to Nelson Rockefeller on policy points, celebrated the galvanizing keynote speech by Walter Judd, and argued among themselves the prospects of Barry Goldwater for President.

When Goldwater put an end to such speculation for the time being by declaring pre-emptively that he would not accept the presidential nomination, and when Walter Judd was passed over for vice president, there wasn't much for the tough young activists to wish for in Chicago, nothing left to do, really, that they cared very much about.

But Marvin's empathy, as always, was hyperactive, and his mind turned, as always, to the need for a fresh organization. Marvin was organization mad. He had set up perhaps two dozen over the years, mostly directed for or against this or the other proposed domestic or international federal initiative. He now sought productive relief and hope for his Chicago kids, and on the final day of the convention, after the vice-presidential nomination was given to Lodge, he said to a knot of them, including leaders Robert Croll and Douglas Caddy, that a conservative student organization should be set up.

Exactly that had been recommended by Goldwater himself to members of Youth for Goldwater for Vice President, which had beat the drums for him at the convention. Why not, said Marvin, come up with a date and a meeting place? He made a phone call and came back to his followers. "Let's go for September 9 at Great Elm, in Sharon, Connecticut. That's the Buckleys'—Bill Buckley's—family home, plenty of room."

The word went out, and a month and a half after the convention, as summer lingered in New England, a hundred young people gathered at Great Elm, where, over three days, they would lay the foundation of Young Americans for Freedom.

2

Young Americans for Freedom

James Burnham lived a few miles south of Sharon, in Kent, Connecticut. He traveled every week to New York City, spending there two vigorous days as a senior editor of *National Review.* He wrote a regular column, a geopolitical review of what he dubbed "The Third World War."

Burnham's reputation as a social theorist had reached an academic and popular high when his book *The Managerial Revolution* was published in 1941. His thesis was that the managerial class had co-opted, or at least inherited, the traditional role in American enterprise of capitalists and owners. From there his attention turned in several books of strategic analysis to the international struggle against the Communists.

For twenty years he had taught philosophy at New York University (he had graduated from Princeton in 1927, first in his class), in many of those years collaborating with Sidney

Hook. Burnham had been a socialist, alongside Hook, but had traveled in the other political direction by the time he agreed to join the fledgling *National Review.*

Burnham was a hard-liner on the matter of the Cold War. He had little patience with accommodationists who belittled the solemnity of the Soviet enterprise. But he was the house moderate in domestic affairs. There had been division, at *National Review,* on whether to support the re-election of Dwight Eisenhower in 1956, the President having recovered from his heart attack and electing to run for a second term. The tough wing at the magazine was led by Willi Schlamm and Frank Meyer, themselves former Communists, and Brent Bozell, a classmate of mine at Yale. They leaned toward a formal break with the GOP, on the grounds that it was deficient in coping with Communist initiatives, diplomatic and military, and derelict in applying conservative doctrine in domestic matters.

Brent Bozell was a rangy, redheaded lawyer, married to my sister Trish in 1949 and already, by 1956, the father of five children. He had stayed on at Yale, after graduating as my classmate and debating partner, to attend the Yale Law School. During his three years in law school in New Haven he coauthored with me the book *McCarthy and His Enemies,* a detailed analysis of the charges McCarthy had made against the State Department. The book argued that, in most cases, McCarthy had been justified.

Brent had been uncertain, after finishing his studies, where to go to practice law, but he finally decided to go to

San Francisco, where he accepted a job at a top law firm. He arrived in California at just the moment that the resolution was introduced in the Senate for the censure of Senator McCarthy. This amounted to a declaration of war against McCarthy and "McCarthyism." It was a corporate dissociation, by a majority of the senator's colleagues, from his entire career as critic and committee chairman.

Bozell's mastery of the near-fathomless McCarthy story brought on a critical phone call from McCarthy's counselor, Edward Bennett Williams, who had tracked Bozell down in California. Williams, the young star attorney in Washington, had undertaken to organize the procedural and—where relevant—legal defense of McCarthy. He asked for Bozell's help, declaring the fight for McCarthy to be nothing less than a matter of critical national importance.

Bozell agreed and moved to Washington, where his performance as, in effect, chief unofficial spokesman for McCarthy attracted wide and admiring attention. McCarthy was censured nonetheless, and less than three years later he was dead. But Bozell, the speechwriter and analyst, had made his mark in the capital.

Having brought his family back from the West Coast, he was prepared to serve as Washington editor for *National Review*. Before long he had caught the attention of Clarence Manion, the law-school dean turned partisan warrior. Manion was incensed at the liberal policies of the Eisenhower administration. It had brought him on board in the early days to serve on a commission to dismantle the Fair Deal, but before long that commission was allowed to die, to Manion's disappointment and anger. In 1959 he conceived the need for a slim book which would give fresh syntactical life to conservative doctrine, to stand in opposition to the prevailing political winds. And who better to serve as the official author than Barry Goldwater, the suave contrarian conservative from Arizona?

Bozell agreed, in June of 1959, to write the book, but his duties on other fronts, especially his duties for *National Review*, imposed delays. He finished the manuscript in January of 1960, and the book was published in April. By the time of the Chicago convention, it had acquired near scriptural authority, especially among the young.

When these young Goldwaterites convened in Sharon in September 1960 to form an organization, the editors of *National Review*—and a handful of older conservatives who had come there, having been advised of this gathering of young conservatives—took no formal hand in their deliberations. But there was close off-hours association among members of three generations.

Meals were served in the great Mexican-style patio of Great Elm for a hundred students, a dozen representatives of *National Review*, and various friends. The elders on the scene included Charles Edison, former governor of New Jersey; authors John Dos Passos and John Chamberlain; and C. Dickerman Williams, legal counsel to *National Review*. Marvin jocularly apologized for his failure to produce Barry Goldwater, and there was much after-dinner speculation—

this was two months before the election—as to whether Vice President Richard Nixon would defeat the fetching young candidate from Massachusetts for the White House.

There was excitement at the end of Day One over the arrival of M. Stanton Evans. He had just been promoted to editor of the *Indianapolis News*, a property of Eugene Pulliam, the press czar whose papers included the two dailies in Phoenix. So Stan Evans, age 26, was the youngest editor of a major daily in the United States. He was also a member of the innermost councils of conservative America.

He was deputized immediately to draft the covenant for Young Americans for Freedom, which he did on Day Two. "The Sharon Statement" comprises a series of clauses, introduced by the words, "We, as young conservatives believe: . . ."

Differences arose on three points. The first was theological: Would the Young Americans acknowledge God, so to speak, by name? That required a vote, and orthodoxy won out: "That foremost among the transcendent values is the individual's use of his God-given free will . . ." Stan was a practicing Christian, though the first chairman of YAF, Robert Schuchman, was a free-thinking Jew.

The second bone of political contention had to do with states' rights, and once again conservative orthodoxy prevailed: "That the genius of the Constitution—the division of powers—is summed up in the clause which reserves primacy to the several states, or to the people . . ."

The sovereignty of a free market also found a place in the Sharon Statement: "That when government interferes with the work of the market economy, it tends to reduce the moral and physical strength of the nation; that when it takes from one to bestow on another, it diminishes the incentive of the first, the integrity of the second, and the moral autonomy of both."

There was much enthusiasm over the accomplishments of the weekend, and the students left Sharon committed to spreading the word in all fifty states. Someone recalled the sentiment, "Oh what a joy it is to be alive and young, with a noble purpose in mind." The ironic quote was from a Communist who had been inspired by his experience with the first Congress of the Soviet Union.

3

Early Days at
National Review

N*ational Review* had been around since November
1955. When the idea gained momentum that a journal
should be launched giving conservative analysis of the events
of the day, the organizers (principally Willi Schlamm and
WFB) were guided by antecedent events in the publishing
life of journals of opinion.

After the war, a group of libertarian conservatives had
collaborated to found a fortnightly, which they called *The
Freeman*. This was done in reverent memory of the legendary *Freeman* that, in the 1920s, had been edited by Al-
bert Jay Nock. The reborn *Freeman*'s founding editors were
successful men of journalistic affairs. Henry Hazlitt was a
prominent author (his *Economics in One Lesson* was a
perennial best-seller), had a regular column in *Newsweek*,
and lectured widely. A story went the rounds some years

after the new *Freeman*'s founding, placing him at dinner with the eminent economist and philosopher Ludwig von Mises, and the novelist Ayn Rand.

Mises was the dean of the Austrian school of economics. Hitler, whom he fled in 1934, must have been the only human being who ever intimidated Ludwig von Mises. He was a mountain of certitudes having to do with the proper organization of economic life. Ayn Rand, born in St. Petersburg on the eve of the Soviet Revolution, was herself a center of social discipline, with whom one differed only at the risk of lifelong excommunication from her kingdom of free creatures who lived by her (their) word, in the creation and re-creation of life, as it emerged in *Atlas Shrugged*.

The story went that at this little dinner, Rand contradicted Mises on some doctrinal point, causing the eminent professor to stop eating and mobilize his scorn and fury on her. Ayn Rand thereupon burst into tears and exclaimed, "You are treating me like an ignorant little Jewish girl!"

Mises jumped up from his chair with joy. "That is exactly what you are! An ignorant little Jewish girl!"

Hazlitt attempted pacification but finally gave up, accepting, as editor of *The Freeman*, occasional essays from the Mises school, as also from representatives of the Rand school of "Objectivism." Years later, *National Review* would publish a critical review of *Atlas Shrugged*, written by Whittaker Chambers. Rand was so enraged by the affront that she cut off all contacts with the magazine and advertised that if ever she found herself at an assembly in the presence of William Buckley, she would immediately leave the room.

Such quarrels did not draw in *Freeman* co-editor John Chamberlain, the tolerant, non-contentious, learned editorialist and book reviewer who had done about a lifetime's work for the *New York Times* and Henry Luce's *Fortune*. He had seen the ravages of factionalism in editorial enterprises.

Also in at the founding, as managing editor, was Suzanne La Follette, a veteran journalist and political activist who many years before had served as managing editor for the old *Freeman*, when it was edited by Mr. Nock.

Before long they were joined by others. There was Forrest Davis, an independent journalist with a long background as a writer for the *Saturday Evening Post* (he published 48 stories there). Davis had edged over in the 1940s toward the libertarian, anti-Communist Right.

And William Schlamm joined their ranks. He was an Austrian Jewish intellectual who, on landing in New York in flight from the Nazis, quickly involved himself in the Luce enterprises. He became an intimate of Henry Luce, to whom he sold the idea of sponsoring a cultural monthly, an idea about which Luce was, temporarily, enthusiastic. When Luce pulled the plug, he left Schlamm without anything at all to engross his enormous appetite for organized editorial life. Ostensibly, age fifty, he was retired, at his house in Vermont (to which he had planned to entice paying guests). He had befriended me, and talked urgently of the need to launch a conservative weekly.

What had happened at *The Freeman* was the overarching lesson for the architectural designers of the projected *National Weekly*, as we originally proposed to call our new magazine. (It turned out the name was taken, and so we changed it to *National Review*.) There had been twenty trustees of *The Freeman*, men successful in their own businesses, with adamant points of view on contemporary politics. When in June 1952 the race for the Republican presidential nomination narrowed to a contest between Sen. Robert A. Taft and Gen. Dwight D. Eisenhower, the Taft men at *The Freeman* prevailed in the matter of whom to endorse. But the dispute had left bad blood between the two sides, and the Ikers withdrew from the magazine. The resulting editorial paralysis led, finally, to the jettisoning of the entire enterprise, deeding *The Freeman*'s corpse to the Foundation for Economic Education, which revived it as an economic journal, dropping the cultural and political commentary that had made *The Freeman* so lively. So that when the time came to organize a fresh journal, Schlamm insisted that I learn from the lessons of the disintegrated *Freeman*: "There can only be a single stockholder," he insisted. And so it developed, in 1955, and so it continued until, fifty years later, I deeded my stock to a trust.

As she had at *The Freeman*, Suzanne La Follette served *National Review* as its first managing editor. After a few years that office went to my sister Priscilla, a graduate of Smith College. She had served as an editor of the college weekly before going to work for United Press in New York and Paris. Willi Schlamm came and very quickly went, a victim of the internecine organizational politics against which he had warned, but to which he ultimately yielded. Willmoore Kendall, too, came and went acrimoniously. He was a professor of political science at Yale, and he had greatly influenced me as an undergraduate. James Burnham, however, came and stayed. He was a veteran academic and a worldly, omnicompetent columnist and editorialist. And soon William Rusher came in as publisher.

Organizational life tends to go rather smoothly, in my experience, when final authority rests in a single hand, though perhaps that is on the order of remarking the stillness in the company of the deaf. Though there were differences, always, in editorial emphases, we were all bound by our attachment to the political claims that upheld the conscience of a conservative. We were especially active in analyzing and projecting policies animated by a determination to frustrate the international Communist enterprise on every front.

Office life at *National Review* was easy-going. But the weekly editorial meeting, at which issues were discussed and editorial assignments made, was fixed: for 10:15 on Tuesdays. The purpose of that hangdog quarter-hour was as explainable as that James Burnham's train from Kent arrived at 10:02 and he had then eight blocks' walk from Grand Central to our offices on 35th Street. The second fixed moment of the week was at 5:45 on Wednesday. What happened then was that the packet containing the editorials written on Tuesday and Wednesday was handed over to the printer's messenger. He would take the train to transport the scriveners' hoard to the giant company in New Haven. H. W. Wilson printed *National Review*—and a hundred other journals—delivering finished copies to us at noon on Friday.

For the editors' meeting, we assembled around the table in my little office (ten years later, we would have a proper conference room). I sat at one end, managing editor Priscilla to my left. Her duties in Paris with United Press had ranged from writing (in French) reports on hockey games to covering the death watch of Marshal Pétain. Before leaving Paris she had been elevated to editor of a news watch, so that she came to *National Review* a seasoned professional, a taskmaster esteemed and, very soon, beloved. She had arrived at the conference, as always, with a tidy list of ten or twenty items for editorial attention.

On my right was James Burnham, pleasant but direct. His voice was professorial, and the words he devoted to his own list of subjects to be explored were neatly framed in his orderly mind.

The participants proceeded around the table, including other senior editors when they were in town. Frank Meyer lived and worked in Woodstock, New York, Willmoore Kendall in New Haven, and John Chamberlain in Cheshire, Connecticut; Bill Rickenbacker was irregularly there, being always at work on several other enterprises. But there were also a few junior editors at the editorial meeting. About ten people managed to crowd around the table.

I having jotted down on a yellow pad the nominated editorial topics, the floor turned to matters of policy, and today
James Burnham wanted to comment on an article in the current issue. It was written by Sen. Harry Byrd, nominally a
Democrat but conceded by all hands to be the most power-
ful conservative voice in the legislature.

Burnham tended to object to ideological superimposi-
tions on factual reporting. "Let me quote one of the senator's paragraphs." For the convenience of those around the
table, all of whom had the current issue in hand, he gave the
page number of the article he proposed to discuss, and
began to read: "'Our free-enterprise system is the greatest
deterrent in the world to Soviet aggression.' He should have
written, 'Our free-enterprise system makes possible our deterrent to Soviet aggression.'

"'It is our first line of defense. Our military forces are
the tools through which the strength of this system is applied in war.' Obviously he meant to say that it is the tools
that do the work in war, but he says it's the 'system.' And
he finishes, 'And our enterprise system can only exist
under solvent government.' That's dutiful canonical language, but of course it's nonsense—we've had deficits
every year now."

"But Jim, what the senator is doing here is just expressing
himself the way they do in the Senate."

"But National Review isn't the Senate."

I turned to Priscilla: "Do senators, when they submit
manuscripts, usually refuse to permit editing?"

"No. Most of them are grateful for it. But in the case of Senator Byrd, we dealt with his A.A., and they're often afraid to authorize any changes."

"That's another reason we need to enhance our reputation. If the speech had been submitted to *The Economist*, they'd simply have made the changes, probably without consulting him."

Priscilla spoke up: "Bill, it's 11:40, and some people are going out to lunch early. Maybe you'd better make the assignments."

These were done. "John, let's give Eisenhower's decision to go to Japan a B treatment." These were codes for the editorial length I thought warranted. Most subjects required only a paragraph's treatment. A lot can be said in a paragraph. Two weeks before, Bill Rickenbacker had written, "They're organizing a paean to Earl Warren next week. People are convening in Washington to paean him."

When the assignments had been made, the editors would file out and go to lunch, or return to their desks, bringing out a sandwich. At the end of the day we worked late, writing the editorials from which I would choose the next evening. Then we would head out to dinner, and this, limited to senior editors and their guests, would be at one of several restaurants nearby. These Tuesday dinners were convivial and relaxed. We retired with the happy feeling that something productive had been done, which would crystallize in the magazine in a matter of hours.

4

An Unwelcoming Committee for Khrushchev

When Brent Bozell wrote the book for Senator Goldwater in the summer and fall of 1959, he was under considerable pressure. Clarence Manion had informed his co-conspirators that he had arranged for a book that would define "Americanism." He had a straightforward political purpose in mind, namely to fortify the sentiment in favor of nominating Goldwater for the presidency in 1960 if possible, or if not that, for the vice presidency. Bozell had no objection to the title Manion had come up with, *The Conscience of a Conservative*, and Goldwater gave his okay. But Bozell's progress on the manuscript was hindered by three factors: (1) his slow writing speed; (2) his duties as Washington correspondent of *National Review*; and (3) his preoccupation, during the summer of 1959, with the immediately impending visit to the United States of Soviet premier Nikita Khrushchev.

Bozell was inflamed by Eisenhower's invitation to Khrushchev and engaged himself wholeheartedly with Marvin Liebman and the community of anti-Communist militants in protesting the first visit to America by a Soviet leader.

President Eisenhower was aware that there was intense opposition to the visit. In due course the photographs of him in the company of his guest were closely scrutinized. It was noted by a *National Review* editor that nowhere in the considerable inventory of photos was Eisenhower seen smiling. An unsmiling Eisenhower was rare, and the protesters took some comfort from the presidential grimness, perhaps brought on in part by the vigor of their dissent.

At one of our Tuesday-evening dinners, *National Review*'s editors explored means of dramatizing the opposition to the scheduled visit. The invitation to the Soviet leader to spend thirteen days in America, including a visit to Hollywood, conveyed—we thought—a kind of conviviality at odds with a correct U.S. perspective on the Communist enterprise.

The following year, when Khrushchev was again to visit the United States, we let our imaginations roam. For that visit, he was scheduled to arrive in New York on a Soviet ocean liner, the *Baltika*. James Burnham, who for all his seriousness of demeanor had a prankish appreciation for the language of protest, either himself suggested, after the wine was served, or else applauded the idea, if it had originated with Marvin Liebman or me, that we figure out a means to dye red the water in the East River into which the *Baltika* would arrive on the mid-September morning.

If the water were colored red, that would certainly attract public attention. I contributed the idea of using the essence put together for small boats in distress that wish to alert rescuers to their whereabouts. It is called "dye marker." A few ounces of it, loosed into the water, create a widening trail of red, expediting identification by Coast Guard vessels or by airplanes miles away. My thought was to empty a quart of dye marker into the East River from the 59th Street Bridge, which would serve to redden the few acres of water through which the *Baltika* would need to plow to reach its designated quay on the east side of Manhattan.

The next day, after consulting the tide tables I kept in my sailboat, I reported ruefully that the current in the East River at the time we would want the incarnadination would be running north from the bridge, toward Connecticut, not south toward Khrushchev. One of us suggested hiring a small airplane of the kind that drags a commercial message through the sky. Burnham got quickly into the question of what text might most dramatically be used, given the requirement of brevity ("Drink Coca-Cola") and urged, simply, "KHRUSHCHEV IS A LIAR." I remember that that struck me as especially adroit, coming from a philosopher and renowned strategist of the Cold War. But we were informed by the little company in New Jersey that mounted air merchandising that an order had come in from the Federal Aviation Agency prohibiting private flights over Manhattan between the hours of 8 A.M. and 12 noon on the critical day.

But, for this first visit of Khrushchev to America one year earlier, our plans were more straightforward: an evening of rhetoric at Carnegie Hall. The house was packed, and eleven speakers registered their protests—among the most eloquent, a woman with a heavy accent who had spent five years in a Soviet Gulag. Bozell was among the speakers, and those of us who knew that as a seventeen-year-old he had won the national American Legion oratory prize were not surprised by his prowess.

We did not succeed in aborting the visit of Khrushchev, but Bozell was now free to turn to the Goldwater manuscript, by now several weeks in default. Four months later he had in hand the 123-page manuscript that shaped the character of the Goldwater movement.

5

Khrushchev
Tours America

*". . . supervision of agriculture and other concerns of a
similar nature . . . which are proper to be provided for
by local legislation, can never be desirable cares of a
general jurisdiction. It is therefore improbable that there
should exist a disposition in the federal councils to
usurp the powers with which they are connected; because the attempt to exercise those powers would be as
troublesome as they were nugatory."*

—Alexander Hamilton in
the *Federalist Papers*, No. 17

*Hamilton was wrong in his prediction as to what men
would do, but quite right in foreseeing the consequences
of their foolhardiness. Federal intervention in agriculture
has, indeed, proved "troublesome." Disregard of the Constitution in this field has brought about the inevitable loss
of personal freedom; and it has created economic chaos.*

WILLIAM F. BUCKLEY JR.

*Unmanageable surpluses, an immense tax burden, high
consumer prices, vexatious controls—I doubt if the folly
of ignoring the principle of limited government has ever
been more convincingly demonstrated. Doing something
about it means—and there can be no equivocation here—
prompt and final termination of the farm-subsidy program. The only way to persuade farmers to enter other
fields of endeavor is to stop paying inefficient farmers for
produce that cannot be sold at free-market prices.*

—The Conscience of a Conservative

Nikita Khrushchev arrived in Washington, D.C., on September 15. Henry Cabot Lodge, the august figure from
Massachusetts, agreed to serve as escort for the Soviet premier. It was one more of diplomacy's paradoxes that Lodge
should be so specially attentive to the national leader of a
superpower noisily determined to undermine Western freedom and to swallow up into Greater Russia as much territory as he could. The warrior Secretary of State John Foster
Dulles was dead now, and his successor, Christian Herter,
was a formalist. A guest of America was a guest of America,
was about as far as he would take it in weighing the matter
of Khrushchev's visit.

No one less urbane than Lodge could have been expected
to live in such close quarters with Khrushchev for thirteen
long days. Moreover, Lodge's mission went beyond mere
diplomatic punctilio. President Eisenhower was a pragmatist,

but also something of an evangelist. In inviting Khrushchev and then consenting to the protracted itinerary, Ike was moved by an overriding assumption: that Khrushchev would be impressed by life in the capitalist world.

Lodge's mind worked quickly. He didn't need more than a minute with the President to get the big picture. He agreed to do the job.

He spent time—Lodge was not a workhorse by disposition—familiarizing himself with the schedule and talking in some detail with the three specialists who would make up his retinue: one scheduler, one interpreter, and one senior member of the State Department's Soviet branch. Lodge added to the staff a personal aide. Harvey Tombstone, never mind the odd surname, did not come from the Wild West. He was a distant cousin of Lodge's, a scholarly young man who, before joining the Foreign Service, had done a graduate paper at Harvard on the Lodge dynasty in American history. An earnest student of the Russian language, Harvey was impressively conversant with the Soviet scene. Lodge, though himself orderly in his life and work habits, quietly enjoyed Tombstone's unfettered ways and would be glad for his company.

Khrushchev's visit would be extensive for the simple reason that the itinerary had to combine what he insisted on and what Washington recommended.

There was New York City, to begin with. Khrushchev would be housed for two days at the Waldorf-Astoria. He would then fly to California on an Air Force 707. Only after Los Angeles and San Francisco would he visit the heartland, specifically Iowa. He would end his trip back east at Camp David, for a ceremonial visit with President Eisenhower.

Settled in New York Khrushchev indulged, on the second day, in a little buffoonery. He strode out twice to the balcony of the lush Soviet consulate on Park Avenue and waved convivially at awed passersby, as if welcoming them to the city. Lodge was not amused by these unscheduled exhibitions. After the second one, he filed an oral protest with Mikhail Menshikov, the Soviet ambassador to Washington. Fluent in English and a specialist in ingratiation, Menshikov coped smoothly with minor diplomatic vicissitudes.

Lodge protested any physical exposure by the Soviet premier save those around which suitable precautions had been taken. "Cabot, do you really mean to tell me it is not safe to look out over Park Avenue?" Menshikov would not let pass an opportunity playfully to touch down on American urban disorder. Lodge let it pass, forswearing references to the more direct means by which the Soviets maintained order. What was more, even Lodge didn't know how many agents were keeping an eye on the Soviet guest. One, of course, would be the KGB's, at the service of Nikita Khrushchev. Then, the agent of whatever Soviets were spying on Khrushchev, and whatever Soviets were spying on the spies who spied on Khrushchev. Lodge would take care to say nothing that got in the way of his antiseptic relations with his guest.

Part of Khrushchev's agenda for southern California was a visit to Disneyland with his family (besides his wife, Nina, he was traveling with three of their children, Julia, Rada, and Sergei, and Rada's husband, Aleksei Adzhubei, the editor of *Izvestia*). But when they arrived in Los Angeles, they learned from Mayor Norris Poulson that U.S. security had flatly vetoed the excursion. The rest of the family could go, but not the Soviet premier. It would be impossible, they were told, in the maelstrom of Disneyland effectively to protect the leader of the Communist world from impromptu demonstrations of some sort by hot-blooded tourists.

Khrushchev objected, but there was no practical means to elevate his protest into a state issue. In the end, his family sullenly joined him on a tour of Los Angeles housing before going on to a luncheon as a guest of Twentieth-Century Fox. This was a star-studded event. Heated applications to attend it bombarded the studio. Everyone seemed eager to attend that lunch—limited, by the size of the dining hall, to four hundred guests, more than had ever before been recorded in Hollywood memory. It would be the same on the following day in San Francisco, where it seemed as if everyone in town expected an invitation from the Commonwealth Club to dine with the Soviet premier.

A feature of the scheduled entertainment at Twentieth-Century Fox was the screening of an upcoming studio release. Selected was the movie musical *Can-Can*, starring Frank Sinatra, Shirley MacLaine, and Maurice Chevalier. The hosts had arranged for a live chorus line to appear on stage to perform their bumptious act. Khrushchev appeared to be enjoying himself. There were photographers there, as everywhere else that Khrushchev traveled, and a spirited cry went up at one point to the dancers to turn about and raise their skirts.

They obliged. Immediately, Khrushchev's party mood changed. He expressed his disapproval, though without any elucidation. But this he provided the very next day in San Francisco, when he met with a group of labor leaders. Khrushchev's reaction was volcanic. "You and we have different notions of freedom. When we were in Hollywood they danced the can-can for us. The girls who dance have to pull up their skirts and show their backsides, adapting to the taste of depraved people. Soviet people would scorn such a spectacle. Showing that sort of film is called freedom in this country. You seem to like the 'freedom' of looking at backsides. But we prefer the freedom to think, to exercise our mental facilities, the freedom of creative progress."

Lodge leaned over to his aide. "Maybe he has a point," he said sarcastically.

Harvey Tombstone whispered back, "Maybe the rear ends at home aren't worth looking at."

"You're supposed to know everything about Russia," the ambassador managed to say, while smiling at a departing guest whose hand was outstretched. "Go find out."

Lodge declined to comment publicly on the premier's tirade. When the reporters were gone and Lodge, bound for the next event, was seated in his sound-protected car with his aide, he intoned, his voice cautiously lowered,

"That was maybe the best example of ignoratio elenchi in recent history."

"What's that?" Harvey cocked his head.

"Don't they teach you anything about logic at Harvard?"

"Well, sir, I guess not. At least, they didn't teach me that—what did you call it?"

"Ig-no-ra-tio e-len-chi. A fallacy. You undertake to refute Contention A by refuting Contention B, with which it is unconnected." But the motorcade's siren sounded now, and Henry Cabot Lodge didn't try to contend with it.

The visit of Premier Khrushchev to the farm in Iowa, scheduled from the outset of his travel plans, was regarded by students of the scene as being of signal importance. One of them cited the importance of Czar Nicholas's visit to Russian farmlands in the west in 1912. Civic leaders hoped the Communist leader would be swayed by this example of the productive advantages of a free market in agriculture.

The preliminaries had been extensive. There had been the coincidental "kitchen debate" in July, two months earlier. Vice President Nixon had been in Moscow to review the U.S. exhibit at the cultural exchange with Russia, a biennial event. Khrushchev himself appeared at the exhibit, without giving notice. He dived for Nixon and engaged in a bout of ideological rodomontade. Nixon avoided the invitation to a generic confrontation, determined to focus proudly on the U.S. exhibit.

What the United States had come up with was a house—an actual house. It sat there in front of them and the surrounding visitors. Nixon asserted that such a comfortable house as they were looking at could be purchased by the typical American family.

The showhouse, brought to Moscow for the exhibit, was full of technological contrivances designed to ease the burdens of life. In the kitchen especially, Nixon pointed out, there were resplendent resources. A refrigerator, a toaster, a washing machine, timers, mixers, all these now proudly itemized by the Vice President of the United States, indicating the virtues of the free world. The camera showed Nixon displaying his palace of appliances to the aspirant leader of the world's working class.

Khrushchev examined it all, and then asked, "Is there also an American machine that puts food into the mouth and pushes it down?" There were guffaws from everyone present who understood the Russian. But now Khrushchev collared an interpreter and brought him to the mike so that everyone could hear in English what the premier went on to say. "We Russians do not focus on luxuries." He waved his meaty hand at the American house. "We think of things that truly matter."

Nixon was silent for a moment but then spoke up, and pointed again to the American house. American technology, he said, is precisely aimed at what matters to "our people and your people." Having the ability to choose what they wish to buy for their own home.

The exchange went on. A visiting American farmer, standing by the press quarters, was especially engrossed.

Roswell Garst was in his fifties, rugged of countenance, his graying hair crew-cut. He gloried in the success of his hybrid corn. And he was scheduled to have a personal meeting with Khrushchev later in the day—part of his ongoing effort, no less, to advance true reform in Soviet farm policy.

Khrushchev had demanded, early in his political primacy—two years after the death of Stalin, whom he had served devotedly—an increase in Soviet agricultural production of an astonishing, and inconceivable, 800 percent within the next five years. An enterprising newspaper editor in Des Moines issued a public invitation to Khrushchev to come to Iowa and see with his own eyes the copious fruits of American agriculture. The editor reminded his readers that before the Revolution, Russia had a farm surplus, which actually allowed agricultural exports, in dark contrast with present-day scarcity.

To everyone's surprise, Khrushchev expressed interest in the invitation and even sent a representative to Des Moines to explore the scene. The Russian emissary was introduced to agricultural enthusiast Roswell Garst. The extrovert farmer persuaded the emissary to recommend, when back at the Kremlin, a personal meeting in Moscow between Garst and the First Secretary, and such a meeting was duly arranged.

Garst was a dedicated American entrepreneur, and when he was ushered into the presence, he was direct, and Khrushchev found him appealing. Garst went on for some time about his corn production, about American livestock, and about the great possibilities of East-West trade. He went so far as to ask Khrushchev how the USSR could know so little about American agriculture, given that Soviets had easy access to U.S. farm journals. Garst permitted himself a little good-natured irony. Inasmuch as the Kremlin had been able to steal the atom bomb from the United States a mere three weeks after we detonated it, why hadn't it succeeded in stealing our means of growing corn?

Khrushchev enjoyed the prod. But he wanted, first, to make a historical correction. It hadn't taken the Communists "three weeks" to steal U.S. atom secrets, he grinned. He raised two fingers. "We did it in two weeks, not three!" He threw back his head and laughed. "You locked up the atomic bomb, so we had to steal it. When you offered us information about agriculture for nothing, we thought that might be what it was worth."

But the next day, Garst was informed, the Soviets ordered an astonishing five thousand tons of U.S. hybrid corn. Garst was now back in Russia, studying the Soviet agricultural scene at the moment when Nixon showed up at the exhibit. He was profoundly convinced that Khrushchev was seriously interested in reform. He was ecstatic when told, a few weeks later, that Khrushchev, planning his trip to America, had asked to visit Coon Rapids.

The manifest of the Air Force Boeing 707 on September 22, 1959, listed as "cargo" the premier of the Soviet Union, his wife and children, and twenty-eight Russian aides. Also in the plane were twelve Secret Service agents. They sat together, except for the two who were posted in the forward-most seats. Some read newspapers, two read books. Two played dominoes.

Amidships, there was a table, convertible for dining or for office use, around which six people could sit. In mid-flight Henry Cabot Lodge's aides sat there—the interpreter, the trip supervisor, and the State Department liaison.

Lodge beckoned to Tombstone to occupy the adjacent seat. Lunch was brought in, steak and macaroni and beans. Lodge tilted his glass for the steward. "I am served a little claret when I am on diplomatic business," he said to Harvey. "That is not a perquisite I share with my aides. In particular not with aides who are only twenty-three years old. But we can share the rest of the meal."

"I wonder what the workingmen's king up there in first class gets to drink."

Lodge closed his eyes briefly, reminding himself that the Air Force plane was secure against electronic eavesdropping. "What do you think he gets to drink, Tombstone? You're a student of Soviet life."

"Well, yes, sir. I assume he's having a snort of vodka. Does the Air Force stock vodka?"

"The Air Force"—Lodge sounded impatient—"stocks airplanes specially for whatever mission is at hand. Today's mission would require vodka."

"If the mission involved a Saudi sheik, and you were squiring him around, would they serve you your claret in his presence?"

WILLIAM F. BUCKLEY JR.

Lodge enjoyed the badinage but thought now to break it off. He turned to a folder and read to Tombstone from the briefing paper. "We land in Des Moines at 6:20 P.M. The premier and his party have the two top floors of the Hotel Fort Des Moines. It happens that a classmate of mine lives near the country club. I have arranged to stay with him."

"But how can you get on without me, sir?"

Lodge smiled. "He has two extra rooms, for you and Antwerp." Antwerp was the interpreter, renowned for keeping silent except when doing his work.

The Air Force jet circled the landing field twice. The tarmac that led to the terminal was bathed in photographers' lights. Two cameramen, one of them speaking in Russian, edged up on the premier and asked whether he had any comment on his mission. Khrushchev said he would wait until the following day to make a statement, after he had conversed with "my dear friend Roswell Garst."

The press was pried away, and Khrushchev was led to his Cadillac. Before he entered it, Lodge spoke: "A satisfactory dinner has been prepared, Mr. Premier, for you and your staff, and of course you can request anything you like"— Lodge managed a smile—"including hybrid corn. I will not be quartered in the hotel, but if you wish to reach me, the security personnel can ring me."

"Have a good evening, Ambassador," Khrushchev said, straightening his tie. "Tomorrow will be an interesting day

for me. And for your tycoon hybrid-corn gentleman." They
shook hands goodnight.

"The whole business is a little out of this world," Alvin
Gray, Harvard 1924, said over drinks. "Khrushchev coming
here to Iowa to find out what the Communists did wrong
when they collectivized agriculture and then attempted
genocide on the kulak farming class."

Lodge shook his finger. The dismissal of the practiced
diplomat. "You don't spend time on the anomalous character of diplomatic initiatives. Even Harvey here knows about
that, and he left Cambridge only two years ago."

Tombstone broke in. "But you're not saying, sir, that the
trip is pointless?"

"Of course not. I'm saying that you don't devote time to
worrying about the concept of it. What we are living out is
an impulse of President Eisenhower and Secretary Herter.
Our job is to go along with it."

Alvin Gray, the banker, asked, "Are you equipped,
Cabot, to answer technical questions about agriculture,
American-style?"

"No. But God knows Mr. Garst is. And anything he
doesn't have the numbers on, we'll get for him—"

"Including a copy of *The Wealth of Nations*?" Harvey
Tombstone interrupted.

"—in plenty of time. He's not going to promulgate a five-
year plan from Garst's farm."

Nikita Khrushchev didn't do that, but the press was prepared for anything. A hundred reporters and photographers greeted Khrushchev's entourage. The cameramen found themselves needing to perch on trees, in barn lofts, at upstairs windows. The crowd made way for Garst's jeep, and Khrushchev and his interpreter got into it.

Followed by a jeep with security men, Garst conveyed the visitors about his farm—a 40-minute drive—telling them along the way about his large-scale planting, harvesting, and livestock-feeding operations. Back at the farmhouse for lunch, they spoke about trade, about arms inspections, and about the ability of their countries to shift to peacetime economics. The premier was genial, especially about Garst's initiatives: "Every conversation I have had with Mr. Garst since 1955 has been important in the build-up for the meeting at Camp David on Thursday."

The meeting in Iowa with Garst underscored the primacy of the political question. That meeting was in September 1959. Khrushchev ordained the Berlin Wall in August 1961. In the summer of 1962 he emplaced Soviet missiles in Cuba, bringing the world to the brink of nuclear war. Soviet agricultural production, meanwhile, fell below the level of 1955 and the advent of Khrushchev to power.

6

Goldwater-Bozell:
Seeking Victory over
Communism

The implications of Khrushchev's visit for public attitudes in the United States, and for U.S. foreign policy, were not quickly probed. The 1960 presidential campaign was about to begin, and of that campaign Theodore White would remark that "rarely in American history has a political campaign discussed issues less or clarified them less."

Goldwater did not train criticism on Khrushchev's visit, in part because it was foreign to his style to disparage any visit by anybody with anybody else. Richard Nixon, moreover, was an enthusiast for the Khrushchev visit, and at that time he was effectively in charge of GOP thinking and GOP policies, and always anxious to dispel suspicions he had aroused in 1948. He had supported Whittaker Chambers, leading some to believe that he was a fanatic on the subject of Communism, paralytically suspicious of the work of its agents in the United States, Alger Hiss being the most conspicuous of them.

As the 1960 campaign swung into high gear, Goldwater conferred with Brent Bozell, his episodic associate and the hidden author of *The Conscience of a Conservative*, which was selling prodigiously. He had in mind, Goldwater told Bozell, a thoroughgoing strategic essay on U.S. policy toward the Soviet Union—a constructive rebuke to the accommodationist line that prevailed in Washington.

Brent agreed to work on the essay after the election, adding that he would want it to be published in *National Review*. He reminded Goldwater that he, Brent, was serving as the Washington editor of *NR*, "and they send me my checks."

Goldwater readily agreed, and told Bozell he thought it would be appropriate to publish the essay soon after the next president was inaugurated. "Whether it's Jack Kennedy or Dick Nixon doesn't matter too much. They're both accommodationists."

Bozell accepted the commission, and what came from it was the most distinctive essay ever written for public consumption on the nature of the Communist threat, and on the corresponding responsibilities of U.S. policy. It was a model of expression, organization, and exhortation.

Bozell sometimes sounded, when he wrote, like Abraham Lincoln. There was the solemnity, the sense of rhetorical architecture, the pleading as from biblical perspectives. Bozell had written an important speech for Senator Joe McCarthy in 1954, arguing against the proposed vote of censure. It had attracted notice by critically sophisticated analysts, one or two of whom had amusingly wisecracked about the vast discrepancy between the idiom of Senator McCarthy, as widely reproduced over the preceding half dozen years, and the syntactical fluency of Senator McCarthy when reciting words obviously composed by someone else.

But the question, Who actually wrote this? was becoming more a matter of curiosity than of criticism, in an age when speechwriters were so widely employed by so many people who aspired for public recognition, whether as the advocate of a political position, or as a candidate, or when giving a commencement speech or a farewell address. Emmet John Hughes, who had served as an occasional assistant to President Eisenhower, later published a revealing book. In it he happily identified the speeches by Ike that he, an alumnus of the Luce publishing conglomerate, had ghosted. Eisenhower was furious when he read the reviews, and denounced Hughes, through an intermediary, as guilty at least of professional infidelity.

The subject of the proper decorum for ghostwriters was briefly examined, and here and there historians continued to identify the men and women who had actually composed this or that speech or memoir. But the consensus evolved that although it was interesting, and even fine, that such as Jefferson and Lincoln and Wilson had composed their own speeches, it was simply the case that the world had changed. Among other things, in the television age everything uttered by a public figure became as of that moment public property, leaving very little incentive to penetrate bureaucratic procedures that guarded the privacy of one's very own word-library. Another point was that professional writers are legion and for hire. Whether individual verbalists went to a political leader because they were attracted to his person, or to his cause, didn't matter. Curiosity ebbed. The biographer might wonder whether Adlai Stevenson's acceptance speech had been written by Adlai Stevenson or by John Kenneth Galbraith or Arthur Schlesinger or James MacGregor Burns, but it was after a while a matter of interest only to specialists. Consider Bozell-Goldwater:

Assumption 3. It follows that victory over Communism is the dominant, proximate goal of American policy. Proximate in the sense that there are more distant, more "positive" ends we seek, to which victory over Communism is but a means. But dominant in the sense that every other objective, no matter how worthy intrinsically, must defer to it. Peace is a worthy objective; but if we must choose between peace and keeping the Communists out of Berlin, then we must fight. Freedom, in the sense of self-determination, is a worthy objective; but if granting self-determination to the Algerian rebels entails sweeping that area into the Sino-Soviet orbit, then Algerian freedom must be postponed. Justice is a worthy objective; but if

justice for Bantus entails driving the government of the
Union of South Africa away from the West, then the Bantus must be prepared to carry their identification cards yet
a while longer. Prosperity is a worthy objective; but if providing higher standards of living gets in the way of pro-
ducing sufficient guns to resist Communist aggression,
then material sacrifices and denials will have to be made.
It may be, of course, that such objectives can be pursued
consistently with a policy designed to overthrow Communism; my point is that where conflicts arise they must always be resolved in favor of achieving the indispensable
condition for a tolerant world—the absence of Soviet
Communist power.

So the paper went, five thousand words of it. It moved at
its own pace, ineluctable, to a conclusion.

History is not the story of the triumph of virtue, though
virtue when properly supported has sometimes triumphed.
The people of the world and their leaders do not rally in-
stinctively behind good causes: if that were true, the
plague of Communism would long since have disappeared
from our planet. They do, however, rally behind good
causes that are energetically and purposively pressed, and
that show promise of winning. If we simply summon the
courage of our convictions, the blessings of a moderately
tolerable life will soon fall on others, as well as ourselves.
And future generations will honor us.

Goldwater followed his own advice to the extent that he could, but in those years there wasn't much opportunity to hew to the hard line. Europe, and the United States, had accepted the wall in Berlin. The U.S.–backed venture to oust Castro at the Bay of Pigs had failed. The talk was of disarmament conferences and cultural exchange. The spirit, indeed the fervor, were there, but Goldwater, as anti-Communist, did not arouse a national movement.

7

Goldwater and
the Labor Unions

Barry Goldwater's national reputation had its roots in his public confrontations with the American labor movement beginning in the late 1950s. Senator Goldwater, as a member of the Senate Labor and Public Welfare Committee, was drawn to the activities of Walter Reuther and his United Auto Workers after hearing complaints about the behavior of the union in Kohler, Wisconsin. That was the home of the Kohler company, which manufactured bathroom fixtures. It was a family company, in something of a company town, of a kind familiar in America in the early twentieth century. Mr. Kohler wished to do everything thinkable for his workers—except let them form a labor union. That was the casus belli, and Walter Reuther was determined to bring Kohler to his knees.

Reuther had become famous for the stiff terms he laid down for the auto manufacturers. They included a demand

for a share of the profits—one-quarter of all corporate profits, he decreed, should go automatically to the workers, via
their union. The proposal was a venture, pure and simple, in
socialist accounting, and Goldwater identified it as such.

Worse, Reuther, through his effective control of the AFL-
CIO's Committee on Political Education, was emerging primarily as an ideologue, not the mere spokesman for the
working class who was renowned for his subjugation of the
automobile manufacturers. Goldwater went to Detroit in
January 1958 to denounce Reuther's use of union funds to
take over the Michigan Democratic Party. He made refer-
ence to Jimmy Hoffa, the boss of the International Brotherhood of Teamsters, who was widely recognized as the chief
larcenist of the trade-union world. But forget Hoffa, said
Barry: "I would rather have Hoffa stealing my money than
Reuther stealing my freedom."

What caught the attention of the public, and of Reuther
himself, was a final line of denunciation improvised viva
voce by Goldwater. His prepared speech, broadcast on
radio, had ended when there was still thirty seconds of air
time left, prompting Goldwater to remark that "Walter
Reuther and the UAW are a more dangerous menace than
the Sputniks, or anything Russia might do."

Reuther, in his own keynote address at a UAW convention,
declared that "Goldwater was a 'stooge' for Republican
politicians and big business" and that he had "undertaken a
campaign of smear and slander aimed at weakening democratic unions everywhere." The trouble with Goldwater,

Reuther summarized, was that he was "mentally unbalanced" and needed a psychiatrist. Reuther liked to blast heavily. He concluded that Goldwater was America's "number-one political fanatic," a "peddler of class hatred."

Although Reuther declined to modify his own denunciations, Goldwater had second thoughts. Of the Sputnik line, he later commented, "If I had to do it over, I never would [have said] it."

But Goldwater was now firmly positioned in the public mind as an enemy of labor-union excesses. In the summer of 1960 his standing as a national figure was acknowledged when a Chicago poll identified him as the furtive favorite for the nomination for vice president.

In the years that followed, Goldwater hotly rejected, month after month, any suggestion that in any formal way he should be considered a candidate for national office in 1964, yet he behaved like a candidate by supplementing *The Conscience of a Conservative* with a broad manifesto of sorts, a two-thousand-word declaration protesting statist answers to social problems. Conspicuous in that manifesto was a condemnation of those labor unions that sought to politicize their economic goals and to undermine the capitalist premises of commercial enterprise.

In a speech to a convention of the National Retail Merchants' Association in New York, he decocted from his declaration a proposal for six labor-union reforms.

He began by drawing attention to an indisputable datum: The power of the labor unions lay in the special protections they had been given in federal and state legislation over several decades. These protections, Goldwater said, needed to be modified. Labor-union excesses had to be recognized as such, and curbed. The rights and concerns of the vital unit in American enterprise—the American working man—needed to be protected.

He proposed six new laws. Together, they supplemented Taft-Hartley's 1947 attempt to redress imbalances in legislation, and they would serve as the backbone of resistance to labor-union excesses for decades to come. They marked Goldwater as the principal "enemy of the working class." Yet he was never taken by serious people as the enemy of the working man. Goldwater's proposals struck most observers of the industrial scene as levelheaded. In the years immediately ahead, several states passed the anchor of his proposal, which was the "right to work" law. It forbade contracts that required employees to join a labor union.

Goldwater's package of laws would have banned unions from excluding workers from membership (which was the equivalent of excluding them from work). And it would have banned unions from using dues for political purposes. It would have required thirty-day notice of a union's intention to strike, and a secret-ballot vote on whether or not to strike upon petition of 30 percent of a union's membership. These items were never adopted by Congress, but they stand as a model of clear thinking about labor law.

The Taft-Hartley Act had been passed in 1947. It had come at the highest moment of postwar labor-union triumphalism. It was passed by both houses, then vetoed by President Truman, then passed again, over his veto. The labor unions declared it a hard national objective to punish all legislators who had voted in favor of Taft-Hartley, most conspicuously, its principal author. The avengers' fight burned most brightly in Ohio, home state of Robert Alfonso Taft.

But the avengers ran into obstacles, chief among them the high esteem in which Senator Taft was held. There was, too, the factor of Mrs. Taft, who had been enrolled as a campaigner, beginning on the very first day of Taft's re-election campaign. "Do you think of your husband as a common man?" a newsman asked at her initial press conference.

"Oh, no," she exclaimed. "No! The senator is very uncommon. He was first in his class at Yale, and first in his class at the Harvard Law School. We wouldn't permit Ohio to be represented in the Senate by just a common man." Taft was handily re-elected.

It was plain, as the years went by, that opposition to excessive labor-union practices was not a mortal position for a legislator. Goldwater's public standing had risen, as also his popularity, and although he downplayed the importance of public-opinion polls, he could not escape publicity given to him in the polls as one of three Republicans who could be nominated for president the next time around.

8

Plotting at Palm Beach

In January 1962 I had a telephone call from William Baroody. It was, he said, a matter of great national importance that I spend Tuesday and Wednesday of the following
week with Senator Goldwater in Palm Beach. Only Russell
Kirk and publicist Jay Hall would be included in the meeting—Brent Bozell would have been invited, but he was in
Spain. I said I could be there but I had a speaking date in St.
Augustine on the first night. Baroody simply repeated that
the meeting was very important.

Baroody was the head of the American Enterprise Institute, a right-wing think tank founded in 1943. We had met
only cursorily, though I knew him to be an influential figure
in behind-the-scenes right-wing politics. He was invigorated
by meetings with small groups, which he much enjoyed
dominating. It was clear that he greatly aspired to be important to Goldwater, and perhaps to a Goldwater White
House.

I was there for breakfast with the other invitees at the imposing Breakers Hotel and, naturally, ventilated the critical point: Were we here assembled to answer Goldwater's questions, or to proffer advice on the presidential campaign two years ahead? If the latter, this had to mean that Goldwater had resolved to enter the campaign, which would be big news: So far, he had steadfastly declined to take that step.

Baroody, by nature domineering, was emphatic on the subject. *Under no circumstances* should anything be said touching on a presidential campaign, inasmuch as Goldwater had not himself decided whether to run and did not want to spend time discussing the point.

Russell Kirk wasn't prepared simply to leave the matter closed. "What is more important," he asked Baroody, "than to try to get Goldwater elected President?"

Baroody was obliged to agree that that would be a wonderful national achievement. "But he has said no."

"They always say no," I volunteered.

"Bill, he has said no on at least five different occasions. If he thought we were going to spend the day on that subject, he would just walk away."

Kirk objected. "I'm the least experienced politically of the people in this room. But I've seen the polls—we've all seen the polls—and Bill has a point: Why should we shrink from telling him that's what he ought to do?"

It required someone of Kirk's arrant innocence in consorting with brute political forces to make his point so insistently. He let go of it only after Baroody promised that he would seek out, some time later, an opportunity for Russell to argue his point personally with Goldwater. "Maybe you can tell him something about William Pitt that will change his mind."

Kirk smiled. "Very well. So what do you have in mind for us?"

"We'll have to coast on that."

Goldwater was in Palm Beach visiting, incognito, with a sister-in-law who was resident there. He arrived at our hotel suite at about 11 in extravagantly informal garb, cowboy hat and dark glasses, a workman's blue shirt, and denim jeans, together with his beloved Western boots. He did bring along a weather-beaten briefcase, though I never noticed his opening it the whole day.

What followed was an hour of general discussion on the policies of President Kennedy and the failure of the Bay of Pigs invasion. Baroody noted Kennedy's surprising drop in the polls: 61 percent of the public thought he spent money too freely, one-third thought him unduly weak in opposing Soviet challenges in Berlin and elsewhere.

Moving on, Baroody brought up the John Birch Society. It was quickly obvious that this was the subject Goldwater wished counsel on.

Russell Kirk, unimpeded by his little professorial stutter, greeted the subject with fervor. It was his opinion, he said emphatically, that the head of the John Birch Society, Robert

Welch, was a man disconnected from reality. How could anyone reason, as Welch had done in *The Politician*, that President Eisenhower had been a secret agent of the Communists? This mischievous unreality was a great weight on the back of responsible conservative political thinking. The John Birch Society should be renounced by Goldwater and by everyone else—Kirk turned his eyes on me—with any influence on the conservative movement.

But that, Goldwater said, is the problem. Consider this, he exaggerated: "Every other person in Phoenix is a member of the John Birch Society. Russell, I'm not talking about Commie-haunted apple pickers or cactus drunks, I'm talking about the highest cast of men of affairs. Any of you know who Frank Cullen Brophy is?"

I raised my hand. "I spent a lot of time with him. He was going to contribute capital to help found *National Review*. He didn't."

Goldwater said he knew nothing about that, but added that Brophy certainly was aware of Goldwater's personal enthusiasm for the magazine and especially for its Washington editor, Brent Bozell—"Why isn't Brent here?" he turned to Baroody.

"He's in Spain."

"Well, our—my—*Conscience of a Conservative* continues to sell."

Kirk said he could not imagine Bozell disagreeing on the need to excommunicate the John Birch Society from the conservative movement.

But this brought another groan from Goldwater. "You just can't do that kind of thing in Arizona. For instance, who on earth can dismiss Frank Brophy from *anything*?"

Time was given to the John Birch Society lasting through lunch, and the subject came up again the next morning. We resolved that conservative leaders should do something about the John Birch Society. An allocation of responsibilities crystallized.

Goldwater would seek out an opportunity to dissociate himself from the "findings" of the Society's leader, without, however, casting any aspersions on the Society itself.

I, in *National Review* and in my other writing, would continue to expose Welch and his thinking to scorn and derision. "You know how to do that," said Jay Hall.

I volunteered to go further. Unless Welch himself disowned his operative fallacy, *National Review* would oppose any support for the Society.

"How would you define the Birch fallacy?" Jay Hall asked.

"The fallacy is the assumption that you can infer subjective intention from objective consequence: We lost China to the Communists, therefore the president of the United States and the secretary of state wished China to go to the Communists."

"I like that," Goldwater said.

What would Russell Kirk do? He was straightforward. "Me? I'll just say, if anybody gets around to asking me, that the guy is loony and should be put away."

"Put away in Alaska?" I asked, mock seriously. The wise-crack traced to Robert Welch's expressed conviction, a year or so earlier, that the state of Alaska was being prepared to house anyone who doubted Welch's doctrine that fluori-dated water was a Communist-backed plot to weaken the minds of the American public.

9

Flying over
the Grand Canyon

Barry Goldwater's charm had a way of imposing itself even on those who were organizationally inclined to resist it.

Five years after the Palm Beach meeting, preparing to travel to Vietnam, I would receive a letter from a young writer whose name I recognized as the co-author of the previous year's political tract, *The Party That Lost Its Head*.

George Gilder and his associate Bruce Chapman were young graduates of Harvard. They were energetically affiliated with the Ripon Society, an assembly of Republicans bent on shaping their party leftward, to keep up with the times. The Gilder book was a scorching, and readable, denunciation of Barry Goldwater and of his campaign for president. It was a plea to lively Republicans to free themselves of the encrustations of the past. Gilder was now doing freelance journalism, and his letter was to ask if I would cooperate with him for a profile in *Playboy* magazine.

He arrived at my apartment, looking as one assumed he had looked all his life: slightly unfocused, dressed as if on his way to class at graduate school, shirt collar footloose, briefcase teeming with journalism and with a paperback classic or two. His manner was that of a diffident researcher, but I knew after reading the book he had written against Goldwater that his prose was not in the least dowdy. It was crisp, here and there lacerating, even a little stentorian.

We spent a half hour and I decided to oblige in the matter of cooperating for a profile. He did warn me—I often reminded myself of this in future days and months—that he worked slowly and that his enterprise would be time-consuming. Indeed it was. In the three months after our initial meeting he came to me in my office and in my apartment, and then to my home in Connecticut, a dozen times. The climax of what had become more nearly a liaison than an interview came in February. He was with me in my apartment at 10 A.M., as scheduled, but he pleaded that although he had worked most of January on his essay, he would need at least two more half-hour sessions to complete the interview. I remember exactly the words that followed.

"George, if you want to interview me any longer, you will need to be on the 3:25 flight to Phoenix this afternoon. I am on my way to Vietnam."

He drew breath, and ticked off one or two questions he had prepared. He left me an hour later and said he would talk to his editor at *Playboy* about his problem. He would call me back to make further arrangements—in March, I assumed. But his call came one hour later. He said that *Playboy* had authorized him to fly with me to Phoenix; would that be agreeable?

My wife and I, followed by George, went down the gangway under escort. It had been commandeered, we quickly saw, by Senator Barry Goldwater, who was standing in his boots and cowboy shirt by his car. He motioned us into his large station wagon. I attempted to introduce him to George Gilder, but the plane engines overhead made this difficult. George and my wife, Pat, were put in the back seat. Goldwater beckoned me up front with him and got into the driver's seat.

Barry had just returned from the Far East, and he talked about problems in Saigon. He told Pat that his wife, Peggy, had drawn up an afternoon schedule for her "which leaves Bill and me time to plot the Cold War." We laughed, and heard, for the first time, the voice of George from the back seat. "Senator, would you let me off at the Mountain View Motel?"

"Why the Mountain View Motel?" Goldwater wanted to learn, touching off the muted horn he had personally devised, loud enough to serve notice on alien company, low enough to comply with Phoenix's municipal rules.

"I'm staying there, Senator. I have a reservation."

"Why are you—" He paused and nudged me with his elbow, whispering to know the name of the young man in the rear.

"George," I said softly.

"George," he called out, "why are you staying at a motel? You can take Barry Junior's room, he's out of town."

The matter was settled, and soon we drove up the steep hill to Goldwater's "Be-Nun-I-Kin," the Navajo phrase for "house on a hill." Goldwater had had the house built in 1957, and for several years it was the only house in the area.

Goldwater assigned my bags and Pat's to the handyman, and himself grabbed Gilder's. "Follow me." He strode across the tiled floor. Gilder looked at me, far gone in what seemed sheer stupefaction.

I reported to Goldwater in his study, teeming with electronic gear. "Barry, have you ever read George Gilder's book, *The Party That Lost Its Head?*"

No, he said. What's it about?

"Well, you. It's an anti-Goldwater-Republican book. He's doing a profile of me for *Playboy* and got an okay at the last minute to come here."

Barry's eyebrows rose. "He seems a nice guy."

I confirmed that he was. "I've seen a lot of him in the last couple of months. He's a very diligent reporter. He's a godson—sort of—of David Rockefeller."

Barry gave a trace of a smile, and then, "Well, Bill, let's talk now about your immediate problems. You go to the Trunk and Tusk Club at 6—they'll pick you up. We'll bring Pat later."

"—and George?"

"And George. Then we'll listen to your talk. After that they'll bring you back here and maybe we can have a high-ball or something. Tomorrow will be"—he smiled fully, mysteriously—"an interesting day, I hope."

The next morning he drove Pat and me and George to the Phoenix airport. We climbed aboard his twin-engined Bonanza. He introduced us rather curtly, I remember thinking, to "Ruth." It irked him that the insurance company was requiring all pilots over the age of fifty to fly with a co-pilot. Clearly there was no limit placed on the age of the co-pilot: Ruth was well into her seventies. She had had a long career as a professional test pilot, but now she was absorbed in her knitting, directing only the occasional word or two to the senator, sitting beside her.

Goldwater flew us to the Grand Canyon, dipping down as deep as the topography permitted. He landed at the air strip near the tourist center. From there a bus took us to the restaurant. Goldwater recommended the Guadalajara Plate. There were scattered questions; some of these had been voiced while we flew, but Barry had not heard over the noise of the engine. One question was my own. "How many times in your flying life have you had to crash-land?"

Goldwater's reply was defensive. "How many times have you, Bill, had a car die on you?"

Twice, I answered.

"Well, I've had two forced landings, and I'm a lot older than you." He paused. He peered out the large window, though it did not serve his argumentative purposes. The view was of the Grand Canyon, where landings of any sort are forbidden.

Over there—Goldwater pointed to a stretch of trees on the way back—over there was where he crash-landed an Ercoupe.

Bits and pieces of the airplane are still cherished by the Hopis as amulets, we learned, and as eternal proof that flying over their territory is forbidden by their earth god.

We finished our lunch and went back to the airstrip, and took off. To the northwest—he pointed—archaeologists have found traces of life dating back before the beginning of Christendom, indicating that the population of northern Arizona was once as great as it is now, when they are charging thousands of dollars per acre. "One day I hope to go back to college and get my degree, and it will be in geology."

We were getting close, and he radioed the tower that he should be landing "in about seven minutes." But there was no airport in sight, and my wife challenged his capricious seven-minute estimate. He accepted the challenge and set the stopwatch going.

Six minutes and 45 seconds later we were within a hundred feet of the runway. He slowed down the plane to stretch out those 15 seconds, but Miss Ruth on the right saw what he was up to and called his game. "You want to reach the field or stall?" she said sternly.

He flashed a determined grin and replied gruffly, unconvincingly, "Shut up, Ruth. Your job is to tell me when we're on the ground." She closed her wrinkled eyelids, and we touched down at exactly seven minutes, without even setting off the stall-warning indicator.

That night my wife and I were guests of honor at a dinner given by Henry Luce and his wife, Clare Boothe Luce. After a long cocktail hour, wine was served at dinner. The waitress whispered to Goldwater, evidently an old acquaintance. She knew he didn't drink wine, so she poured him a discreet whiskey—and then another.

It was a long evening, and when Mr. Luce asked me for my thoughts about Vietnam, I replied that we'd surely be better off hearing from Senator Goldwater, since he had just returned from there. I felt a wince of shame, I later confessed to George, at having put on the spot a sometime presidential candidate who had every reason to be groggy from glass after glass of whiskey. But Barry Goldwater rose, spoke for eight or ten minutes, and gave the twenty guests an analysis that I thought lucid and penetrating, and which proved prophetic.

The next morning George Gilder rode to the airport with Pat and me. He was heading east to New York, Pat and I west to Los Angeles, where she would visit her sister while I went on to Saigon. Stepping out of the car, Gilder stopped, his bag in hand, and turned back toward me. He hesitated for a moment, and then said: "I'm glad I didn't have this experience of knowing Goldwater before writing my book."

10

Internal Strife: The Baroody Factor

In 1962, Brent Bozell moved his family to Spain. He was keen to give thought to a politics that he deemed theologically informed. In 1966 he would found, with his wife, Patricia Buckley Bozell, the magazine *Triumph*, which sought a political reading of the Christian faith.

But in the summer of 1963 he returned to the States and turned his attention back to the U.S. domestic front, anticipating Barry Goldwater's race for the White House. Brent had stepped down as a senior editor of *National Review*, but he now resumed close contact.

In what seemed continuous conversational exchanges with Frank Meyer and James Burnham, the idea developed that there was intellectual amplitude out there unperceived, let alone satisfactorily integrated. The ongoing challenge was to encourage a broad, culturally appealing conservative GOP. At

National Review we were in touch with a community of conservative-minded scholars in fields relating to foreign policy and, especially, Soviet/Marxist cultural challenges. Meanwhile, on the political side, the name of Goldwater figured prominently, in *National Review* and in syndicated columns written by me and a half-dozen others.

Brent suggested a concrete organizational step. Goldwater, he had concluded, needed a committee of scholars who would publicly identify themselves with the cause and associate themselves with him as the principal political spokesman of that cause. In an hour we assembled a list of several dozen political scientists, economists, and journalists we thought approachable. We were ready to discuss the proposal with Goldwater, and I phoned down to his Washington office for an appointment.

What we got, in a suite in the Hay-Adams Hotel, was a meeting not with Goldwater, but with Jay Hall, Denison Kitchel of Phoenix, and, of course, Bill Baroody.

We made the case for setting up a pro-Goldwater committee of intellectuals and were met with formal enthusiasm. But also with a kind of corporate reserve—which Bozell, who only three years earlier had given Goldwater the manuscript of *Conscience*, found bizarre, as did I after a long period as friend and occasional advisor to the senator.

Goldwater was supremely important not only on the political scene, but also on the collateral intellectual scene. Owing to *The Conscience of a Conservative*, to the running endorsements of *National Review*, and of course to his own singular talents as a speaker and political diplomat, he had emerged in 1963 as the senior conservative political presence in the United States. That designation withstood the test of time. Thirty years later, the historian Matthew Dallek wrote in *The Atlantic Monthly*, "The year 1960 brought a turning point for the conservative movement. That year Barry Goldwater published *The Conscience of a Conservative*. Generally dismissed in the national media, the book stands today as one of the most important political tracts in modern American history." Another historian (Mary Brennan in *Turning Right in the Sixties: The Conservative Capture of the GOP*) would later write: "*Conscience* altered the American political landscape, galvanizing the right and turning Goldwater into the most popular conservative in the country."

But in the fall of 1963, Goldwater Inc. was floundering. "Was there ever such a politician as this?" Patrick Buchanan, the young Republican professional, asked in disbelief. "*The Conscience of a Conservative* was our New Testament. It contained the core beliefs of our political faith, it told us why we had failed, what we must do. We read it, memorized it, quoted it. For those of us wandering in the arid desert of Eisenhower Republicanism it hit like a rifle shot." But how diligently, and with what political perspective, was this development being greeted?

I had copied out for the benefit of Goldwater the hagiographic citations of his book and the eager explorations of what might lie ahead. But he wasn't present at the Hay-Adams; so I handed them to Bill Baroody.

The committee of intellectuals we had in mind would bolster Goldwater's standing as the continuing vessel of activist leadership. But even after an hour of laudatory discussion of the idea, neither Baroody nor Hall nor Kitchel showed himself moved to concrete action. The project would need financing, however modest, but that presumably would not have been difficult to find. Bozell was available to organize the committee, but there was no conversation about commissioning him. And so we left Washington for the air shuttle with some bewilderment.

We reached LaGuardia late and walked to the car Bozell had parked in mid-afternoon. The motor was running—he had forgotten to turn off the ignition. I fought off the lure of a metaphor for the entire day. Instead, I just checked the gas gauge, anxiously.

The shot across our bow came one week later in the *New York Times*, a story under the headline "Random Notes from All Over: Goldwater Aides Counter Right / Rebuff Overture by Buckley, Ultra-Conservative Editor." There was a photograph of me, no mention of Bozell. The article contained the sentence: "The Goldwater-for-President ship has just repelled a boarding party from the forces who occupy the supposedly narrow territory to the right of the Arizona Senator."

The story line should have been transparent, but neither Brent nor I, in our innocence, had grasped it. Some years later, in his biography of Goldwater, Lee Edwards analyzed the rebuff at the Hay-Adams and the *New York Times* story. He wrote,

> Who leaked the "boarding party" story? It could not have been Buckley or Bozell, badly damaged by its misleading contents, or Hall, so concerned about secrecy that he would turn on the radio during meetings to deter bugging. It could not have been Kitchel, who did not know a leak from a leek and who in fact assured Buckley that he had not talked to anyone, let alone a reporter from the *New York Times*. That left Baroody, who, when questioned, suggested that the room had been bugged but who, in the opinion of Goldwater, Kitchel, and Buckley, was himself the culprit.

Although Goldwater later claimed that he would have welcomed them with open arms, Buckley, Bozell, and Rusher were all prevented from making any significant contribution to the 1964 campaign. Describing them as men "of the highest integrity and solid conservative views," Goldwater acknowledged that they should have been able to talk with him and others in the campaign about issues, strategy, the media, and other matters. In his 1988 memoirs, the senator comments, "Later, realizing what had happened, I was heartsick about the matter. But what could I say? What could I do? It was too late."

In fact, Edwards wrote,

There were several things he could have done to involve (1) the man who wrote the book that helped make him a national political leader, (2) the editor of the most important conservative journal in America, and (3) the man who had been instrumental in creating the Draft Goldwater Committee, without which the senator would not have been nominated for president. He could have asked Bozell to research and write speeches; he could have melded Buckley's contacts with Baroody's list to produce an outstanding academic committee; he could have directed Kitchel and Dean Burch, who was hired in September as Kitchel's administrative assistant, to include Rusher in their strategy sessions. But he did none of these things, offering only the unconvincing excuse that it was "too late."

11

"Barry's Going to Run"

I didn't know Denison Kitchel except as, from time to time, we converged at conservative meetings or rallies. We had taken a liking to each other, and Kitchel sent in regular financial contributions for the maintenance of *National Review.* I remember telling Brent that if there had to be a number-one insider on the Goldwater scene, I'd nominate Denison Kitchel—"though Bill Rusher says he [Kitchel] doesn't really know anything about politics." We all assumed that Clif White, who had headed up the Draft Goldwater Committee, would be Goldwater's campaign manager if he ran.

"What *does* Kitchel know about?" Priscilla asked.

"Well, obviously he knows how to be a friend and confidant of Barry Goldwater. Of course he's an important lawyer in Phoenix, and he studied at Yale and at Harvard Law School. He had a large hand in Barry's campaigns for the Senate and, before that, local stuff."

"That doesn't get Goldwater any closer to the White House," Rusher said, and we agreed.

But it was only the next week that the message came in. Would I lunch with Kitchel in New York?

"That's obvious," I said to my secretary, Gertrude Vogt. "Yes. Where? When?"

"He suggested the Century Club."

"I'm not even a member. I assume he is."

"That's where he suggested. Any time the first week of October."

Kitchel was an imposing man, diffident in manner yet direct. He came quickly to his mission, preceding it with, "Let me say that I trust you."

"Well, thanks."

"And I didn't like the turn of your last visit, with Bozell, to Washington."

I paused. "I didn't much like it either."

"I have one thing I want to set right today. And that's, well, you and Goldwater. I don't want that turn of events to alienate you."

I was surprised. I had no palpable sense of alienation from Goldwater, though I had reason to feel alienated from the movement to get him nominated. But the early stages of that movement—before Baroody took it over—had been substantially in the hands of Bill Rusher and Clif White.

"Here's what I have to offer you in earnest money. The best-kept secret in the house."

"Barry's going to run?"

"Yes. But even he doesn't know it for sure. But I know it because I know him. But if a single nightingale in the press says Goldwater has decided to run for president in 1964 what will happen is that he'll maybe even leave the country to emphasize that he isn't going to do it."

"How do I persuade you that I won't leak what you tell me?"

"By giving me your word."

"Is it okay to ask you what brought him around?"

"Yes. He really wants to campaign for President against John F. Kennedy. He likes Kennedy, but he thinks he's wrong on basic issues and that he—Barry—is the best man to make that case publicly. But Bill, that's just between us. I don't want to talk any more on that theme. Talk to me about Cuba. About Castro. About Yale."

"You can talk to me about Harvard."

"Yeah. But I won't. I left there a long time ago."

12

The Conscience of a Conservative

Robert Edwin Thomas had agreed to preside over the evening. But he wanted to hear from Kitchel exactly whose idea the seminar was. Already Goldwater had hinted that, if nominated, he would name his old friend to a senior role. Kitchel told Thomas he was especially anxious to probe the basic question: Could the campaign succeed in popularizing the libertarian precepts of Goldwater's book?

"Who I *don't* want invited," said Robert Thomas, "are political passersby who figure it would be instructive or entertaining or even memorable to spend an evening listening to Robert E. Thomas expound on educational philosophy as seen through the eyes of our man of the moment, Barry Goldwater."

The middle-aged GOP staffer David Steinberg, himself a PhD before turning to politics, not only agreed to comply with the legendary old man's stipulations, he also affirmed his agreement with them. He had spent too much time at fund-raisers, too many hours addressing listless men of affairs, many of them having wan reserves of intellectual energy, to submit willingly to more of the same. What he had in mind specifically for the evening's seminar was something on the order of analysis and instruction for carefully selected guests. The goal was to explore the public communicability of Goldwater's program.

Robert Thomas was an enthusiast for *The Conscience of a Conservative*. He profoundly believed that a failure to take the work seriously would damage the strategic prospects of the Republican Party. A former congressman and senator from Ohio, Robert Thomas cared deeply about the party. When he was defeated for re-election to the Senate in 1956 he returned to the practice of law without complaint, with his door always open to serious students of politics. There was an encouraging number of these, men and women who venerated his mind, envied his experience, and admired his facility of expression.

Kitchel had hired the private dining room of the Governor Calvert House in Annapolis. It had room for sixty guests, at ten dining tables. When the evening's guest list was assembled, pared down, added to, it included two senators, six congressmen, and a half dozen major GOP contributors. And there were eight journalists and authors.

At the front of the room was a screen, easily seen by the guest seminarists. Senator Thomas turned his wheelchair to face the screen and with his right hand moved the material he wished to consider so that it would be visible on the screen. The evening's topic would be the chapter in Goldwater's book on the subject of education.

"I am much taken," Senator Thomas began after perfunctory opening remarks, "by the lucidity of the thought in the passages we'll be looking at. They are from his book, of course, and though they dealt with legislation that Congress was considering five years ago, in 1959, the analysis might as well have been of the pending education bill, which simply projects the thinking of the 1959 act.

"I urge careful attention to what I have called the lucidity of the exposition. Here is a prime example of what can be accomplished in political exegesis, because it instantly advises that an orderly mind is at work. We know, most of us in this room, that Barry is perfectly capable of going on too long and getting lost, and wasting time in dialectical highways and byways, but he is also, at his best, an expositor of thoroughbred skills." The room was gratifyingly still.

"But as you have been warned, my purpose is to devote the hour exclusively to his chapter on education. It is the 9th chapter of his book, the last of the chapters taking up domestic questions. He ends the book, quite properly, with a chapter called 'The Soviet Menace.' The chapter we're talking about, 'Some Notes on Education,' ends a conspectus of essays. They begin with 'The Perils of Power,' pass by states' rights, civil rights, the problem of the farmer, of the labor unions, of taxes and spending, and of the welfare state in general.

"I don't propose to take you line by line through his notes on education, though were I to do so, I would lengthen the evening by not more than a second hour. The economy of expression in Goldwater's survey of the subject gives pleasure in proportion as the public has suffered from the disorderly prose our public figures imposes on us, and I readily admit that I have myself been responsible for a share of this.

"Anyway, let's begin."

There was a murmur of excitement. Thomas, the teacher, could do that to people. "Goldwater acknowledges the public concern for education, or, more properly, the lack of it . . ."

I agree with lobbyists for federal school aid that education is one of the great problems of our day. I am afraid, however, that their views and mine regarding the nature of the problem are many miles apart. They tend to see the problem in quantitative terms—not enough schools, not enough teachers, not enough equipment. I too think it has to do with quality: How good are the schools we have?

"That is a straightforward introduction to the subject— inferior education—immediately followed by the distinction between the uninformed critics, and . . . us, the rescue party."

Their solution is to spend more money. Mine is to raise standards. Their recourse is to the federal government.

Mine is to the local public school board, the private school, the individual citizen—as far away from the federal government as one can possibly go.

"Again, note the distinction. But note also the rhetorical melody—short sentences, eminently quotable, even easy to commit to memory; all of it infinitely useful to polemicists at work, giving short talks at rallies, writing quick notes to constituents. And of course note the monitory flag—the warning against turning the whole mess over to federal agencies, which is what we have substantially been doing for over a decade.

"Yes?"

Steinberg, seated at the speaker's side, whispered to him an identification. The questioner who had raised his hand was Allan Finlay, influential young congressman from California.

"Senator Thomas, I can understand Goldwater's clinging to the private sector as the preferable way to go. But does it make sense to deprecate automatically the public sector in the way Goldwater does? Or is he going to make the . . . desirable . . . discrimination later on?"

"Wait a bit, Mr. Finlay. And tell me later if you think the objection you make is insufficiently coped with.

"So, with your permission we move on to a fateful note."

And I suspect that if we knew which of these two views on education will eventually prevail, we would know also whether Western civilization is due to survive, or will pass away.

Senator Thomas leaned his head back and let silence reign for a few seconds. "There, a whiff of apocalypse. A whiff. Just that, no more.

"Goldwater moves on to give reasons for his alarm. As he puts it, there are . . ."—Thomas's pointer moved on the screen—

. . . four reasons why federal aid to education is objectionable even if we grant that the problem is primarily quantitative.

The first is that federal intervention in education is unconstitutional. It is the fashion these days to say that responsibility for education "traditionally" rests with the local community—as a prelude to proposing an exception to the tradition in the form of federal aid. This "tradition," let us remember, is also the *law*. It is sanctioned by the Constitution of the United States, for education is one of the powers reserved to the States by the Tenth Amendment. Therefore, any federal aid program, however desirable it might appear, must be regarded as illegal until such time as the Constitution is amended.

"Oh Christ!" That came from a guest at the far end of the room. "I mean," the protester explained, "the Tenth

Amendment plea is what conservative politicians do when they are desperate . . ."

"Yes." Senator Thomas was unfazed. "And in the context you invoke, a lot of *The Conscience of a Conservative* is out of this world. But hear Goldwater out:"

The second objection is that the alleged need for federal funds has never been convincingly demonstrated. It all depends, of course, on how the question is put. If you ask, Does State X need additional educational facilities? the answer may be yes. But if you ask, Does State X require additional facilities that are beyond the reach of its own financial means? the answer is invariably no. The White House Conference on Education in 1955 [found that] . . . "No state represented . . . has a demonstrated financial incapacity to build the schools they will need during the next five years." . . . My view is that if State X possesses the wealth to educate its children adequately, but has failed to utilize its wealth for that purpose, it is up to the people of State X to take remedial action through their local and state governments. The federal government has neither the right nor the duty to intervene.

Someone in the room, without intending his comment as a question for Thomas, said that it didn't make much political sense to hold local school boards responsible as they were de facto unaccountable. Thomas nodded—he had heard the point—but moved on.

I asked Mr. Arthur Flemming, the Secretary of Health, Education, and Welfare, how many of the Nation's school districts were in actual trouble—how many, that is, had reached their bonded limit. His answer was approximately 230. Now there are roughly 42,000 school districts in America. Thus, proponents of federal aid are talking about a problem that affects only one-half of one per cent of our school districts! . . .

This may be the place, while we are speaking of need, to lay to rest the notion that the American people have been niggardly in support of their schools. Since the end of World War II, Americans have built 550,000 classrooms at a cost of approximately $19 billion—almost all of which was raised at the local level.

Thomas raised his hand to acknowledge the questioner in the front row. He repeated the question so that everyone could hear it, then nodded and said, "Wait a moment, sir. Goldwater immediately comes up with the data you want to see."

Here are some of the figures. In the school year 1949–50 there were 25 million students enrolled in various education institutions in the United States. In the year 1959–60 there were 34.7 million—an increase of 38%. During the same period revenues for school use, raised largely at the local level, increased from $5.4 billion to $12.1 billion— an increase of 124%. When school expenditures increase three and a half times as fast as the school population, I do not think that the adequacy of America's "traditional" approach to education is open to serious question.

"Goldwater feels the need for data at just the moment I, as a listener or reader, feel the need for them. And he goes on to satisfy that need. Let's continue:"

The third objection to federal aid is that it promotes the idea that federal school money is "free" money, and thus gives the people a distorted picture of the cost of education.

"This, in my judgment," Thomas froze the text on the screen, "is a supremely important point. Goldwater goes on to illustrate the reach of that delusion, right to his home town."

I was distressed to find that five out of six high-school and junior-college students recently interviewed in Phoenix said they favored federal aid because it would mean more money for local schools and ease the financial burden on Arizona taxpayers.

The truth, of course, is that the federal government has no funds except those it extracts from the taxpayers who reside in the various States. The money that the federal government pays to State X for education has been taken from the citizens of State X in federal taxes and comes back to them, minus the Washington brokerage fee. The less wealthy States, to be sure, receive slightly more than they give, just as the more wealthy States receive somewhat less.

But the differences are negligible. For the most part, federal aid simply substitutes the tax-collecting facilities of the federal government for those of local governments. This fact cannot be stressed often enough; for, stripped of the idea that federal money is free money, federal aid to education is exposed as an act of naked compulsion—a decision by the federal government to force the people of the States to spend more money than they choose to spend for this purpose voluntarily.

The guests were silent. And attentive.

"Are you ready for his fourth and final objection?" There was the consent of the silent.

The fourth objection is that federal aid to education inevitably means federal control of education. . . I do not question the desirability of encouraging increased proficiency in the physical sciences, but when the federal government does the encouraging through the withholding and granting of funds, I do not see how it can be denied that the federal government is helping to determine the content of education; and influencing content is the last, not the first, stage of control.

Nobody should be surprised that aid has led to controls. It could, and should, not be otherwise. Congress cannot be expected to appropriate the people's money and make no provision for how it will be spent. Congress would be shirking its responsibilities to the taxpayer if it distributed his money willy-nilly, without regard to its use. . . . Congress will always feel impelled to establish conditions under which people's money is to be spent, and while some controls may be wise, we are not guaranteed against unwise controls any more than we are guaranteed against unwise Congressmen.

Steinberg raised his hand to say, "Goldwater sounds here as though there was no educational problem out there. If we endorse that position at the convention in San Francisco, we'll run the risk of being run out of town."

Thomas looked at his notes and conveyed instructions to the screen. "Here is how Goldwater handles that point."

Note that I have not denied that many of our children are being inadequately educated, or that the problem is nationwide. I have only denied that it is the kind of problem that requires a solution at the national level. To the extent the problem is quantitative—to the extent we have too few classrooms and pay some of our teachers too little money—the shortages can be taken care of by the localities concerned. But more: to the extent the problem is qualitative—which in my opinion it mainly is—it is manifestly one that lends itself to correction at the local level. There is no place where deficiencies in the content of an educational system can be better understood than locally, where a community has the opportunity to view and judge the product of its own school system.

In the main, the trouble with American education is that we have put into practice the educational philosophy expounded by John Dewey and his disciples. In varying degrees we have adopted what has been called "progressive education."

"Senator, if Goldwater here—I haven't read *Conscience*—is going to take on the whole question of modern education, I'm going home. After all, I wrote an entire book about defective modern teaching—"

"And I've read it." Senator Thomas turned his eyes right and left. "Our guest is a prophetic writer on the subject. Mortimer Smith's work is no doubt known to all of you. It is certainly known to Goldwater, especially *And Madly Teach*. But let me go on." There was a murmur of approval.

Subscribing to the egalitarian notion that every child must have the same education, we have neglected to provide an educational system which will tax the talents and stir the ambitions of our best students . . .

In our desire to make sure that our children learn to "adjust" to their environment, we have given them insufficient opportunity to acquire the knowledge that will enable them to master their environment.

In our attempt to make education "fun," we have neglected the academic disciplines that develop sound minds and are conducive to sound characters.

. . . Most important of all: in our anxiety to "improve" the world and insure "progress" we have permitted our schools to become laboratories for social and economic change according to the predilections of the professional educators. We have forgotten that the proper function of the school is to transmit the cultural heritage of one generation to the next generation, and to so train the minds of the new generation as to make them capable of absorbing ancient learning and applying it to the problem of its own day.

The fundamental explanation of this distortion of values is that we have forgotten that purpose of education. Or better: we have forgotten for whom education is intended. The function of our schools is not to educate, or elevate, society; but rather to educate individuals and to equip them with the knowledge that will enable them to take care of society's needs. We have forgotten that a society progresses only to the extent that it produces leaders that are capable of guiding and inspiring progress. And we cannot develop such leaders unless our standards of education are geared to excellence instead of mediocrity. . . We should look upon our schools not as places to train the "whole character" of the child—a responsibility that properly belongs to his family and church—but to train his mind.

Our country's past progress has been the result, not of the mass mind applying average intelligence to the problems of the day, but of the brilliance and dedication of wise individuals who applied their wisdom to advance the freedom and the material well-being of all of our people. And so if we would improve education in America—and advance the fortunes of freedom—we will not rush to the federal treasury with requests for money. We will focus attention on our local community, and make sure that our schools, private and public, are performing the job the Nation has the right to expect of them.

Senator Thomas turned his wheelchair to face his guests. "That's the essence of it."

Steinberg asked, "And you think analysis of that order won't shock—won't dismay—the delegates at San Francisco?"

"Look, David, if you had asked me four years ago, Should Barry Goldwater publish this manuscript? I'm afraid I have to tell you I'd have said: No. There's too much purist conservative doctrine in it, and you can't just jettison ideological and political accretions of thirty, forty years.

"But what happened is he *did* publish it and it has made U.S. publishing history, selling three and a half million copies and turning all eyes on him among wistful—and adventurous—Republicans. And I'm betting that the kind of deliberation we gave his chapter on education here tonight predicts the kind of thoughtful reaction to the whole book we can expect from a wide range of people. Our challenge, this year, is to appeal to the conservative conscience of America."

An aide responded to the signal and edged the wheelchair toward the elevator. The guests clapped, and Robert Thomas bowed his head in acknowledgment.

13

In the Snows of New Hampshire

Senator Norris Cotton was too often passed over as just one more granitic export from New Hampshire. But he was never dismissed by his colleagues. Barry Goldwater perceived early, and accurately, that Cotton had achieved his standing by exercising unusual powers of discernment and diplomacy.

Cotton was therefore not surprised when Goldwater, in mid-December, formally requested an hour with him. The date was made. They would meet at Cotton's office (#428 United States Senate Office Building, not distant from Goldwater's #317).

Cotton's private office was spare and unremarkable, excepting the huge deer head and antlers looming over the framed American flag brought from Iwo Jima by Cotton's nephew. Cotton was himself born on a farm in New Hampshire. He had been elected to the New Hampshire State

Assembly at age twenty-three, one of the youngest legislators in history. His closest friend and lifetime companion had been Styles Bridges, his fellow Republican and adamant conservative, sometime president pro tem of the Senate, dead in 1961.

"Barry," Cotton said in his blunt way, immediately after Goldwater sat down, "you want to talk to me about running for president. I'm glad you changed your mind. It sure took you a long time."

"Well, yes. Actually, Norris, you got anything to drink? I'm shy, and that would make it easier."

Cotton laughed and reached into the little bar under the bookcase. "Barry, if you're here to ask me if I'll back you in the primary in New Hampshire in March, I have a quick answer for you."

"Not too quick if it's going to be negative, Norris. Give it to me slowly."

"No. I'll speed it up and just say—yes."

Goldwater showed his pleasure, and tipped his glass to his lips.

"But there's one thing. Styles is gone, so we won't have him to pave the way locally. That means we've got to talk it over with some of the state party people. And we'll have to tiptoe our way around the widow: Doloris Bridges plans to run for Styles's seat, did you know that?"

"I guessed it. That's gotta mean she's turned down an offer to serve as Chairlady of the John Birch Society."

"Yes, there's that problem. No doubt about it." He paused. "But, well. When are you going to announce?"

"I was thinking January 3."

"You want me there?"

"Norris, I'm going to announce in Phoenix."

"Good idea. They have good weather in Phoenix." Norris Cotton pursed his lips. "Not like New Hampshire."

"No, not like New Hampshire. I was there a lot for Nixon in the '60 campaign. But describing the weather in New Hampshire is—I guarantee you, Norris—the unfriendliest thing I'll ever say about New Hampshire during the primary. And I won't say it again, but—thanks."

They talked about the days ahead.

After surgery to remove a calcium deposit, Barry Goldwater's right heel had been slow to mend, and he had to cope with the walking cast in New Hampshire's snow. He had never dealt with snow as a sheer factor in getting about. His campaigning for Nixon had been in the leafy fall.

Norris Cotton had prescribed an itinerary that took Goldwater from city to farmhouse to hamlet, slogging the whole way, accepting any useful help—including, more than once, a sled of sorts on which he was able to kneel.

"There's no way you can get away with spending less time in New Hampshire than Nelson Rockefeller," Cotton said, driving from the Concord airport. "Among other things, Bill Loeb wouldn't like it if he thought you were short-changing New Hampshire."

William Loeb was the owner, editor, and publisher of the *Manchester Union-Leader*, the newspaper that covered—smothered—the state of New Hampshire. The paper was unrelievedly right-wing, and Loeb insinuated his likes and his dislikes into every page. He received at his office, ceremoniously, every candidate for statewide and national office without ever suggesting that he would defer other than to his own predispositions, and perhaps those of his wife, Nacky, on the matter of endorsements. "Rockefeller has already called on the old dragon," Cotton said.

"Maybe Governor Rockefeller has offered to build New Hampshire a new statehouse. Nelson would annex New Hampshire, if he could."

"It's not that easy to buy the state, Barry. There's a strict limitation, in New Hampshire, on political spending. But Rocky is working hard and has plenty of young volunteers—Dartmouth types. I take it for granted that my old school, Exeter, will also field some Rockefeller troops. On the other hand, Barry, you're pretty strong with the young folk. For some reason. Well anyway . . . I have Exeter and Dartmouth on your schedule."

"Can you program me to avoid Doloris?"

"Not likely. She's everywhere. Mrs. Styles Bridges, Mrs. New Hampshire. And of course she knows GOP history backward and forward. I've seen her a lot on the news. She seems to have memorized everything you ever said or wrote. Which, Barry old pal, is not the best news in the world."

Barry groaned. "Oh God." He had said a thing or two in his career that he didn't like to recall. Like his temptation to lob a nuclear bomb into the men's room of the Kremlin.

The primary voting date was March 10, and Goldwater had scheduled twenty-one days in the state. Night after night, while Goldwater was on the road, or briefly back in Washington, his closest aides met, usually in a hotel suite nearby. Richard Kleindienst and Denison Kitchel, Dean Burch and Karl Hess. They would convene at the designated debriefing site, in a suite vacated for the evening by the Goldwater-for-President people.

Cotton sat at the head of the table, or whatever served for a table in the makeshift room. He was a most fastidious man, and the Goldwater staff deferred to him routinely. Denny Kitchel would report the political news as seen, or digested, from his own redoubt, usually in Manchester or Concord or Nashua. Three subordinates, variously located, knew which number to call to give local news. There was only the one New Hampshire television station, broadcasting from Manchester, but several channels came out of Boston, and they covered the New Hampshire primary profusely.

Burch read aloud from the notes he had taken on the telephone. Television was unsparing in its coverage of the campaign. It seemed sometimes as if the whole of the State of New Hampshire was involved, man, woman, and child, in the Republican primary. Camera time was given not only to

Rockefeller and Goldwater but also to prominent endorsers. Senator William Knowland had come in for Goldwater from California, also John Tower and Peter O'Donnell from Texas. All of New York's Republican congressmen dutifully supported their governor, Nelson Rockefeller.

Burch went on: "Doloris, you'll all be pleased to hear, gave an interview in Franconia. She said that Rockefeller"—he looked down at his notes—"had a soft—s-o-f-t—record on Communism. But hang onto your hats. She then said, 'The man is not a Communist, at least I don't think he is.'"

Nobody spoke. Cotton raised the subject of Governor Scranton and the universal attention being paid to him, notwithstanding that he said repeatedly he was not a candidate for president.

"You ask me?" Karl Hess came in. "Candidate for president? That's exactly what he is. To run, all he has to do is, simply, be the Anti-Goldwater."

"But that's what Rockefeller is," Kleindienst objected.

"Yeah I know. He's certainly the obvious 'other' candidate, but there's a little bit, in Rocky, of yesterday's news. Scranton is fresh."

Senator Cotton raised his hand. "Here is the schedule for tomorrow." He said where everyone was to go, and where their evening meeting would be held on the next day.

Ten days later they met at Benton. There was snow and grit on their coats, but the routine was unchanged. Kitchel opened by giving news about the groundswell for Henry Cabot Lodge. "Son of a bitch is sitting under palm trees in Saigon. Figure out how to maneuver to do that during a New Hampshire primary and you belong in the White House."

"Let's get on with it. Dean, we'll hear from you."

Burch would go down his notes, as always. There had been a favorable editorial in the *Concord Monitor*. A delegation of students from Dartmouth had picketed the Goldwater speech in Nashua. A roving television camera had pursued Doloris Bridges all day in Nashua. Goldwater had been asked, in Rochester, whether he would have approved using federal troops to enforce integration in Little Rock. Mrs. Bridges had spoken to the Ladies' Club at Claremont and said that the whole world should be grateful to Goldwater for "penetrating the Social Security fraud." Earlier, in Laconia, she had complimented Goldwater for remarks made two years earlier questioning the reach of the U.S. military.

"Karl, you have something for us?"

"Yes. Mrs. Bridges gave another interview. Two local stations picked up that Barry is 'against' Social Security. Against. The *Concord Monitor* features her saying that Barry would end TVA and get the U.S. back on the road to military power. She reminded the reporter that Barry had said he'd like to lob a bomb into the men's room of the Kremlin. She said that was the way it should be."

There was silence.

It was stunning.

"We couldn't believe it," Burch said later to a close friend. "But that's what happened. Senator Norris Cotton said nothing. Then he reached under the table to his brief-case and brought out a bottle of Old Crow. He put it down on the table in front of Kleindienst.

"'Richard,' he said, 'you must go fuck Doloris.'

"We couldn't even look at Dick's face. We just went down to the bar."

14

Ebullience in California

It was a big race—Bill Rusher employed a lascivious enunciation when making this point—"a *very* big race." Rusher, who had conspired since 1961 with Clifton White in a small group determined to draft Goldwater, was present at Memorial Hall, Stanford University, representing, unofficially, the little clutch of Suite 3505 insiders who had worked to capture the convention delegates who would decide, in July, whom to name.

The 3505 operation sought to work behind closed doors. But the laws of creeping recognition did not spare them. You could not realistically hope, in an age of modern communications, forever to hide the existence of such a political operation. It was bad enough that Goldwater had taken frequent opportunities, as 1963 wore on, to deny that he sought the nomination, and even to hint that he would reject it. But he couldn't make 3505 just go away. Here was a group of affluent, successful men who, though they numbered less than one hundred, could reasonably hope to influence the Republican Party's choice for president.

F. Clifton White was the small group's dominant member, known widely in the political world as the soft-spoken, lyrical wizard from New York with intuitive powers of organization. He had a record of successes in local and regional enterprises—accepting challenges, and upsetting the odds.

They called themselves "Suite 3505" because they wanted a meaningless designation that could serve as something of a fingerprint that would get communications to their votaries placed on top of the pile of mail on executive desks. "Suite 3505" was simply the two-room office in New York City whence they operated. Bill Rusher had proposed the address, and no one objected.

William A. Rusher was a political activist, abundantly qualified. He was—to begin with—the publisher of *National Review*, and had been so almost from the beginning of the journal's life. I had initially taken on that job myself, serving as both editor and publisher. But then I spotted a hugely engaging stretch of polemical prose, signed by William A. Rusher, identified as special counsel to the Senate Internal Security Subcommittee under the formidable Senator James Eastland. I dug a little and learned that Rusher had graduated from Princeton, gone off to war, and returned to enroll in the Harvard Law School. On graduating, he joined a blue-ribbon law firm in New York but after seven years took a leave of absence to serve in Washington on the subcommittee, which investigated various Communist fronts and fellow travelers, notably the Reverend Martin Luther King Jr.'s associate Hunter Pitts O'Dell.

Rusher, who was and would remain a bachelor, was super-articulate, persuasive, and determined. Although his job with the magazine was nominally full-time, he was forever involved in political operations and ad hoc committees advancing conservative causes and candidates. In 1964, he harnessed his full energies to help Goldwater win the presidential primary in California in June. I, skeptical about Goldwater's chances of beating Nelson Rockefeller, had casually mentioned to my colleagues at *National Review* that if Goldwater lost in California, the magazine should proceed in its editorial deliberations on the assumption that the nomination in San Francisco would go to Rockefeller. That impiety, uttered in his own precincts—moreover, by the man who had the simple authority to set policy for the magazine—so distressed Rusher as to cause him to spend a week on the ground in California, observing the insidious work of the opposition, and invigorating the loyalists to work even harder.

The 1964 California primary was an extravagant affair. It would cost more money than some recent presidential campaigns. In play, for one thing, were the resources of Nelson Rockefeller. They were copious. The self-designated "moderate" wing of the GOP was substantially endowed, with hard cash and credit. Rockefeller's California operation had been much cheered by the victory of their candidate in Oregon in May, and by the backing of several major California dailies.

But Goldwater had his own troops, and they were resolute. They were unregimented and uncoordinated, yet massive. Volunteers were everywhere, doing everything, indeed inventing things to do. A harried Goldwater staffer said of them that they "ran through the woods like a collection of firebugs." They would light many fires, at rallies, going from door to door, meeting outside schools and department stores, writing letters to newspapers. Such fires sometimes had to be doused, as when one young matron in Costa Mesa wrote a letter to the editor explaining how Goldwater's character would be an advantage in any prospective nuclear engagement. "*Nuclear engagement!* Shut that woman up!" barked Clif White, who had finally been brought into the official campaign.

But spontaneous contributions could also be ingenious and useful. And the cast was eclectic. From Hollywood came two doughty conservatives, Ronald Reagan and John Wayne, proclaiming their faith in Goldwater. Phyllis Schlafly was apparently no more than a housewife in Alton, Illinois, for all that newspaper coordinates would reveal. But, mother of six, she was an effective drillmaster with singular ideas on how to serve her cause. A decade after the Goldwater campaign she would go on to mastermind the defeat of the "Equal Rights Amendment." This proposed amendment (#27, it would have been), advertising women's rights and civil equality, would have brought on an avalanche of lawsuits, on everything from unisex restrooms to young women being subject to conscription.

Schlafly had been on Goldwater's bandwagon early on. She had been on the committee headed by Clarence Manion when he published *Conscience*. Her idea of an appropriate contribution to the California contest was a slim book exposing a few "secret kingmakers" based on the East Coast. She pictured them as mischievous socialist-minded folk who sought to debauch national independence by excessive federal spending and thoughtless foreign entanglements. All of this would weaken America in the enduring contest with the Soviet Union. She placed not a single ad for her book, *A Choice Not an Echo*, but a record-setting six hundred thousand copies were in circulation by June 2, when the California voters went to the polls.

The Speaker of the Stanford Political Union wore black tie, as was the custom. He stood on a small platform tucked behind the heavy wooden lectern. F. D. Rico (Franklin Delano Rico) was a New Yorker whose parents for many years did day work on the Hyde Park estate where President Roosevelt was born, where he weekended when governor, and where he came for visits by private train when he was president. Young Rico never laid eyes on the great God of the Hudson Valley. But even close contact with FDR would not have made a significant impression, since Rico was only one year old in 1945, when the president died.

After Roosevelt's death, the Ricos, mother and father, were kept on—he was a handyman; she cleaned and washed—and in due course their son went off to boarding school in nearby Millbrook, New York. His given names embarrassed him when he went to school, and he considered amputation, which would have freed him to pursue life under the name "Franklin," or even "Frank." But home for the weekend he caught the sheer suffering in his mother's eyes at the prospect of deracination, and he eased back into the Franklin Delano Rico he had grown up with.

What he did not preserve, at Millbrook, was his inherited political faith. To his parents' dismay, he was converted by his roommate, Hamilton Fish IV. The senior Fish had been the Republican congressman for that district since what seemed the beginning of time. Indeed, Congressman Fish was the single legislator whose voice, the day after Pearl Harbor, had been heard on the radio when President Roosevelt asked Congress for a declaration of war against Japan. Fish had been a stalwart noninterventionist, and he succeeded in getting in a few seconds ahead of the President to observe that as far as Congressman Fish was concerned, attempting to destroy the United States fleet at Pearl Harbor overrode any previous recommendations of the need to pacify Japan.

Arrived at Stanford in 1960, the young FDR eagerly involved himself with the student Republican Club and took part in debate tournaments, gaining respect for his versatility and wit. In May 1963 he was elected Speaker of the Political Union, never mind the jokes about the ensuing need to cut down the height of the lectern—FDR was only five feet four inches tall. When he campaigned for Speaker he passed around buttons stamped FDR IS TALLER THAN NAPOLEON.

Nobody denied that, on his feet debating, or presiding over an affair at which there were other speakers, he made his voice heard, and his rulings were clear and persuasive. Patronizing Franklin Delano Rico was done at user's risk.

Now he banged his gavel on the lectern. He had arranged with Salvatore—the college electrician, with whom he conversed in Italian—to wire the overhead lights to a switch that lay on the lectern. FDR didn't like to use this Father of All Lights, and had done so only once, when silence was critical because of the student who had been injured when he was pushed over the guard rail of the balcony by an exercised partisan. Rico had no intention of using this ultimate weapon at the big debate. Unless, of course, it became necessary.

The Speaker's problem in inducing silence took a new turn when he spotted, marching down the center aisle toward him, the four young women. Each bore a one-word placard, the four adding up to:

STANFORD

VOTES

FOR

BARRY

Then the music began.

The scene gave the impression that the whole of Stanford University was a music school. Filing into the hall were trumpets and drums, French horns and flutes, piccolos and violins, playing the theme of Schubert's *Unfinished Symphony*, as other students sang:

> *Bar-ry is going to win,*
> *Is going to win the nom-i-na-tion.*
> *Bar-ry, we love you so*
> *We love you so because—you're Bar-ry . . .*

The Youth for Goldwater having made their point, Rico returned to the gavel:

"Ladies and gentlemen, this is a discussion society, not a music hall. . . Yes?"

"Point of order."

"The rules," Rico nodded, "do not permit me to fail to recognize a member pleading a point of order. So yes, proceed."

"Mr. Speaker, it is wrong—discriminatory—unconstitutional—shameful—to have permitted a demonstration for one candidate and not for his opponent—"

"I would advise the gentleman from the Liberal Party that the demonstration was not officially planned; the Speaker was not consulted about it; and if the Rockefeller forces had come into the hall with an equivalent demonstration, I would not have interfered with them—"

"*Let's get on with the program!*"

"I agree with that voice from the Party of the Left. We will proceed.

"I have a few introductory remarks.

"We are all aware that the vote on Tuesday, four days from now, will register a political note that will be heard around the world. Uh—yes? The gentlewoman from the Party of the Right?"

"Mr. Speaker, why debate something we have been hearing both sides of day and night for the last three weeks? Mr. Speaker, may I ask a personal question?"

"Well," said FDR, "I'm not sure that would be appropriate. If the question pertains to personal information not in keeping with the proper business of this meeting, how could I then undo the damage?" There was laughter, and a clapping of hands.

Another voice from the rear. "*Call the Rules Committee.*"

Rico looked about at the assembly of a thousand students and at the bank of television cameras and radio mikes. "I rule that the gentlewoman with the personal question should submit it to the Rules Committee tomorrow, and that the committee should advise me of the ruling in time to discuss it at the next meeting."

There was a roar of approval.

"So . . . as I was saying, the results of the vote on Tuesday are of national, even international, importance. Under the circumstances, I request the Stanford Union speakers to use their allotted time prudently—"

From the rear: "*Prudence sucks.*"

Rico banged down the gavel. "We will get on with the program. As you know, we will have, in the formal program, only a single speaker on either side; then there will be questions. We will hear now"—Rico stole a glance at his notes—"from Elizabeth Quennell, for the Liberal Party. Miss Quennell."

There was loud clapping from half the hall. The other half stayed silent—there was no booing, booing being contrary to the rules of the Union.

Elizabeth Quennell was a twenty-year-old junior majoring in sociology. Her blond hair was neatly knotted at the back of her head. She walked a little nervously to the lectern, and then pulled a few pages from her notebook, adjusting her glasses. She devoted three of her allotted ten minutes to the personal background of Nelson Rockefeller. She spoke of his career as a student at Dartmouth, of the volunteer work he had undertaken, the two summers spent in slum work in Cincinnati and then in New York. Of his work for President Roosevelt in Latin America—"Es un señor que habla español como indigeno," which got her a smattering of applause from the few dozen Hispanic students. And then of his rise through the ranks in New York to become governor. "Think of this historically. Governor Al Smith." Applause, mild. "Governor Franklin D. Roosevelt." Tumultuous applause. "Governor Averell Harriman." Applause.

"I recognize the point of order." Rico pointed his hand at the questioner.

"What about Governor Tom Dewey?" There was a clamorous agreement on the point raised.

Elizabeth Quennell replied: "Mr. Speaker, why should I mention manifest failures? I am talking about governors who *deserve* applause."

The house was confused by this bifurcation. There was laughter and finally applause.

"I'm talking about great names in New York history positively *overtaken* by Nelson Rockefeller, who leads the fight today in California to give the country someone of his stature and sophistication.

"Mr. Speaker, the case for the affirmative is made as simply as by citing *The Conscience of a Conservative*. This Child's Tale of Politics has a certain dreamlike fascination, appealing to fundamentalists—"

Speaker Rico pre-empted the dissenters with a light bang of the gavel.

"But we cannot send out as the presidential candidate of the Republican Party someone who believes that"—Quennell drew out a slender book—"'The government must begin to *withdraw* from a whole series of programs that are outside its constitutional mandate—from social welfare programs, education, public power, agriculture, public housing, urban renewal and all the other activities that can be better performed by lower levels of government or by private institutions or by individuals.'"

There was a muted cheer from the Party of the Right. Then applause and rigorous questions. And, finally, Rico introduced Jonathan Purcell, who spoke for the Negative, opposing the endorsement of the Rockefeller candidacy.

"Mr. Speaker," the slim, boyish student, wearing tortoise-shell glasses and a blazer, a blue shirt, and a red and gold tie, said confidently, "let's take up the argument right where the

Liberal Party's representative led us. She asked were we willing to do without the programs undertaken by the federal government under a franchise she defended. She listed social welfare, education, public power, agriculture.

"Isn't it time"—he raised his eyes, which traveled from the left of the hall to the right—"that we use our powers of analysis? These have been wonderfully fortified at this great institution, founded by an enterprising individual, a Californian, who less than eighty years ago began with buildings that had a combined capacity almost exactly equal to this single hall. Was this in any way a state enterprise?

"I speak of our powers of analysis. In reciting all those government activities praised by the Affirmative, it is only left to ask, as Senator Goldwater did in his book, 'What if the resources taken for the public sector were left to us to dispose of?'

"Mr. Speaker, I paid—my father paid—tuition and board for one year at Stanford last September. The grand total was just less than two thousand dollars. But an additional eleven hundred dollars can be traced to—government. Gifts to Stanford—to Miss Quennell and to me—from state and federal governments.

"Am I glad to have had this subsidy? Yes, I am glad. But if we prosper at Stanford from government largesse, who is responsible for it? Somebody paid for it. Who? Why? It is of course we—my father and yours—who benefit. Senator Goldwater says it shouldn't be so, that the money for all these grand things should be generated from private gifts and from tuition, as was true at Stanford seventy years ago. I and every member of the Negative, I am certain, pledge here and now to endeavor in our lifetimes to make gifts the equivalent of our subsidy, if the government would just let us alone, if the government followed the prescriptions of Barry Goldwater in his *Conscience of a Conservative* as, I pray, the whole nation will do if only we give it a chance."

The speaker received an ovation.

A speaker for the Rockefeller faction announced that there would be a "Rally for Rock" on Monday evening at the Main Quad before the big vote on Tuesday.

It seemed that everybody in the whole world was involved in the California primary contest. Yet the central figure, if only for that day—May 31—was Nelson Rockefeller Jr., weight 7 pounds 10 ounces. There was no way to keep news of the birth from the voters, nor to bury completely the recognition of the infidelity that had brought it about. On Tuesday, June 4, Rockefeller received 1,052,053 votes, Goldwater 1,120,403.

15

Rockefeller Looks Ahead

Nelson Rockefeller was handed the early edition of the newspapers, all of them giving first attention to his defeat. The defeat was bad enough, but he was angry over the prominence attached by so many lead writers and columnists to his new wife, Happy, and the birth four days earlier of their child. ("I want to call him Nelson," Happy had insisted. "Just so you don't call him Barry," Nelson replied. Happy laughed, and Nelson reflected for the thousandth time why that woman had been nicknamed "Happy" when she was a mere girl. She made everyone, and everything, happy, just by virtue of whatever it was that came out of her.) Henry Easton, in his syndicated column, said that the closeness of the vote in California (Goldwater, 1.12 million, Rockefeller, 1.05 million) very simply verified what George Hinman had predicted, that "there are people out there who don't want someone who has divorced and remarried to live in the White House." This meant that Nelson couldn't plausibly tell Happy, let alone his campaign associates, that the remarriage and the birth of Nelson Jr. had no bearing on the political development.

At breakfast that morning with Hinman and Jack Fuller, the talk turned first to the California vote. Rockefeller had a rule in these matters, which was that no time at all would be spent on what had been done, or what had failed to be done, unless there was direct bearing on the scene ahead. For instance, after polls in Oregon had seemed to verify that the voters there weren't in favor of a constitutional amendment to permit prayer in the schools, Rockefeller had encouraged talk about what emphasis to place on that question in California, where he would begin the primary campaign the following week.

But today there was no primary campaign left to plan. This fact, again, Rockefeller wished to adduce, in a tone of voice that discouraged any talk about problematic futures ("What if Goldwater . . .").

But he not only authorized a different kind of talk about his future, he dived right into the subject. "As you know, gentlemen, I am determined to serve as president of the United States."

Yes, George and Jack knew this, but would not have raised the subject the morning after his defeat in the critical primary. He had a fear most immediately communicated, in those days, by the mention of the name of Harold Stassen. In 1948, as former governor of Minnesota and as president of the University of Pennsylvania, Stassen had campaigned for the Republican nomination. He was, in fact, an early favorite, until his debate with Thomas Dewey, which had simply destroyed Stassen in everyone's estimation except Stassen's. In 1952, when Dewey was out and the race had narrowed to Eisenhower vs. Robert Taft, Stassen entered several primaries, with virginal enthusiasm. In 1960, Stassen yet again submitted his name, which however was taken up only by the nation's comics. Johnny Carson said that Harold Stassen was campaigning for citizenship in Minnesota, and everybody laughed.

"None of that kind of thing for me," Nelson Rockefeller told himself. He was comforted by two factors. The first was that he was still the governor of the state of New York, and apparently unbeatable—he would be elected to that office four times, finally quitting undefeated. That—and he was enormously wealthy. He could have been rich as Croesus and without any prospect whatever of political success. But there was nothing in his nature to foretell sheer political impotence. His station in life was that of a winner. Yes, he had missed out on the presidential nomination in 1960—hard to beat an incumbent vice president. But now in 1964 he was at it again. Why should he yield to superstitions about creeping immobilization when the data continued to build up on the other side? Look at Ike!

He could absolutely trust the men with whom he shared breakfast this day. So he said to them: In order to forget yesterday, let's look ahead.

"Now, one thing is absolutely certain: Barry is not going to win the election in November. A victory for Goldwater is simply inconceivable. If I had won the GOP nomination, there'd have been a ghost of a chance I'd go on to win, even against the memory of JFK, but not Barry, not with his voting record."

He rather liked Barry Goldwater. They breakfasted together from time to time, and were able to talk about other things than their contentions in New Hampshire and California. Even though Goldwater had prevailed this time around, that was hardly disqualifying to Rockefeller in the future of the GOP. Yes, taxes had risen in New York—but in election after election, the voters of New York had sent Rockefeller back to Albany. They were evidently willing to make the sacrifice of higher taxes in return for what higher taxes had brought them. No one was seriously critical of his administration's investment in New York State's infrastructure—the new and refurbished highways, the integration of the public universities, the environmental protection, the regulation of business. There was trans-ideological opposition to his tough drug laws, but they would not cost him GOP support. On the contrary. He was a tough law-and-order man.

So, he permitted himself to think out loud, we'll back Goldwater heavily during the campaign. I mean—he smiled—"half-heavily." His public criticisms of Goldwater during the primary campaigns weren't on issues Lyndon Johnson would press. Who cared that Nelson had warned against "extreme-right" support? Everybody warns against extreme-right support.

What would Nelson's criticisms of the John Birch Society do? The Society had been run out of town by *National Review* in 1962, so what could that waning organization of kooks do to Rockefeller in 1968?

Yes, he had charged Barry with being insensitive to opportunities for international cooperation. But was anybody going to be mad about that, four years from now? On foreign policy, Nelson was an anti-Communist, "and so is Barry. He knows that, I know it, the voters know it. It isn't as if I've said he was begging for nuclear war. That's one for the Democrats to charge, not us."

"So what are you going to say publicly, Governor?" George Hinman, the suave, aristocratic political diplomat, always used the title in personal conversations with Governor Rockefeller.

"I'll congratulate him, of course, and say how important it is to watch for the vainglory of Lyndon Johnson and his appetite to take over all social services for all of America.

"That sort of thing. Don't you agree?"

Hinman always agreed with the governor.

16

Goldwater's Youth
Movement

The senior staff of *National Review* hadn't scheduled a
formal meeting to give attention to the upcoming Republican platform. But it was on everybody's mind, even
though, as with most political platforms, it would end up
mostly as ideological chimera combined with populist
rhetoric. What had hung in suspense no longer did so.
After California, it was known that Barry Goldwater, not
Nelson Rockefeller or William Scranton, would be nominated for president.

But it mattered that there was continuing, even harden-
ing, opposition to Goldwater's voting position on the Civil
Rights Act then before Congress. Only five other Republicans had announced their opposition to the bill, which
would come up for a vote later in June.

It was Tuesday evening, and we were seated around a table for six at Nicola Paone's quiet, tidy, and succulent restaurant. But Brent Bozell wasn't there. "Never mind," Priscilla said cheerfully—she brought cheer to all subjects, every day, every week. "Brent's always late."

Bill Rusher, the outspoken publisher of *National Review*, was a man of regular habits. Consulting his mysterious notebook with its unfathomable resources, he easily checked back on attendance records at the preceding editors' dinners. He reported that Brent had almost always been a half hour late. "Accidentally, he is sometimes on time."

"While on the subject of Brent," I intervened, "let's remember that he goes out of his way to avoid public mention of the hand he had in writing *The Conscience of a Conservative*—"

"The 'hand'?" James Burnham interrupted. "He even wrote the typos."

"He doesn't deny it. I mean, Brent doesn't deny it," said Frank Meyer, reigning ideologue and close friend of Brent's. "He just sort of avoids mention of it. This is—or should be—a ghostwriter's code."

"If that's how Frank puts it, that's the way it is." I was referring to the reliability of Frank's word in the matter, given the legendary frequency of communications between Bozell, in Washington, and Meyer, in Woodstock, New York. Theirs was an unending campaign to purify conservative thought, a topic of amusement among their colleagues. "An emergency phone call from Frank Meyer to Brent Bozell," Willmoore Kendall had once remarked, "is defined as a phone call that interrupts the regular phone call from Frank Meyer to Brent Bozell."

We were interrupted by the materialization of Bozell, who joined the group eagerly.

I had assigned, for the next issue, editorial discussion of the GOP platform, with special attention given to the subject of civil rights. "That," Burnham said, "is Goldwater's principal vulnerability—"

"—apart from President Lyndon Johnson." Rusher produced his characteristic aside.

"Yes," Brent nodded. And, with mock concern, "Lyndon Johnson *is* in the picture on election day."

President Kennedy in November, just seven months ago, had reshaped the political horizon by falling prey to the assassin's bullet in Dallas. The unencumbered ascendancy of Johnson was a deeply felt geopolitical event. The assassination had initially brought on a reconsideration by Goldwater of his decision to run for president. It hadn't been until December 8 that he finally told his closest associates that, yes, he would run.

President Johnson was in the White House as the constitutional successor to the martyred president. But he was there, besides, as agent of something like a sacramental commission to take on, much further than had been planned by Kennedy, the undefined mission of the Kennedy Administration—and to redesign the face of the Old South.

The Democrats' leverage in Congress had been achieved, over several decades—including the decade of Franklin

Delano Roosevelt—by the most artful dissimulation in American political history. The Democratic Party was hailed as the party of reform, of social conscience, the progressive vessel of a modern and permanently altered nation born with the New Deal. For two decades the Democrats' life and strength had depended critically on the party's hold on the U.S. Senate. And this had been effected with the compliance of a dozen Southern senators given power by the rules of seniority. And all of them were agents of the Jim Crow Southern tradition.

What they faced now, with Lyndon Johnson reborn, was a looming transformation by the Civil Rights Act. In the spring of 1964 it lay in the bowels of Congress like a fetus teeming with life, but not yet quite born. It was ardently backed by President Johnson, whose backing was all the more eloquent for his historical identification with anti-civil-rights legislative and executive devices. But today he was the principal champion of a bill that would assert a federal right to seek out discrimination in every quarter of Southern life and to harness the dormant engines of the federal government to fight such discrimination. It would bring to life equality before the law in the little courthouses in the South which, pleading states' rights, had for so long devised means of frustrating the liberal passions of the high-minded.

"I'm not going to plead scriptural authority for *Conscience*, but let me quote a couple of lines from it," Brent said at dinner.

"Good," Priscilla nodded. "I have to admit I haven't read it since January 1960, though I've read everything Brent has written since then."

"All of it improved by your editing," Brent lifted his wine glass. "Okay. So these are the lines from *Conscience* I want to remind us of:

"'A *civil* right is a right that is asserted and is therefore protected by some valid law. It may be asserted by the common law, or by local or federal statutes, or by the Constitution; *but unless a right is incorporated in the law, it is not a civil right and is not enforceable by the instruments of the civil law.* There may be some rights—"natural," "human," or otherwise—that *should* also be civil rights, but if we desire to give such rights the protection of the law, our recourse is to the legislature or to the amendment procedures of the Constitution. We must not look to politicians, or sociologists—or the courts—to correct the deficiency.'"

Burnham tapped on the table. "My own view of it, on the distinction you make, is that you, and Goldwater, were right as a constitutional matter. And we know that opposition to the act on constitutional grounds is a major contention of Goldwater's lawyer in Phoenix—William . . ."

"Rehnquist." Bozell supplied the name.

"Yes, Rehnquist. And we know that Barry is inclined to vote against it when it reaches the floor this month. There are two questions: (1) do we urge Goldwater to vote against it? And (2) what stand do we take on the vote of the platform committee? Do we urge it to evaluate the Civil Rights Act as the act is weighed in *Conscience*, as unconstitutional? Do we hold that the San Francisco convention has a responsibility to honor the constitutional analysis of *Conscience*? Or do we advise it just to ignore that analysis?"

Frank Meyer, who had fought a thousand parliamentary lost causes to the end when he was an official of the Communist Party, raised his hand. "Look, we know the Civil Rights Act will have been passed by the time the GOP meets in San Francisco. We are all therefore bound by the letter of that law, and Barry has said he too would be bound—"

Brent interrupted. "We're not going to influence the vote. But our job—right, Bill?—is to guard the distinctions."

There was scattered talk. Burnham suggested: "Maybe we're best off recommending to Goldwater that he waive constitutional objections, in pursuit of whatever harmony we can get in San Francisco. After all, one day after the platform is accepted, they're scheduled to nominate Goldwater for president."

Brent spoke. "On the practical question, one more sentence from *Conscience*."

I raised my hand and there was quiet. "Go ahead, Brent."

"Barry writes, 'It so happens that I am in agreement with the *objectives* of the Supreme Court as stated in the *Brown* decision. I believe that it *is* both wise and just for Negro children to attend the same schools as whites, and that to deny them this opportunity carries with it strong implications of inferiority.'"

Burnham had been a professor of philosophy for many years. He said now, "Brent, that's some nice prose from Goldwater, but it has nothing whatever to do with the question we're talking about."

"Okay," Brent said. "Okay. So Bill will decide how to phrase our misgivings. Good luck, Bill."

I acknowledged my authority by ordering another bottle of wine.

17

The Campaign Strategy

"The right wing might as well just take over Disneyland!" Harvey Tombstone was off duty, but had decided to attend the Goldwater rally at the Herbst Theatre in San Francisco. He passed his eyes over the program as the band played exuberantly and the overflow crowd stirred, the police struggling to keep the mob outside in order.

He began to chuckle, and before long his merriment was out of control. Marvin Liebman, who had gotten a seat for Lodge's aide, tried to quiet him. But soon Harvey was back at it. "It's the sheer impudence of it all!" he grinned, tears of laughter on his cheeks. "*Chiang Kai-shek . . . Taylor Caldwell . . . The House Committee on Un-American Activities . . . George Sokolsky . . . Herbert Kohler . . . National Review . . .* And in case anyone misses the point, who to give the benediction? *Father Halton!*" Father Hugh Halton was the Catholic priest at Princeton whose excoriations of the Left had become so shrill that the bishop had finally had to quiet him.

Tombstone, always the researcher, was off again. "Virtually the entire contemporary demonology of liberalism. Every one of them, right here. And not to be burned at the stake, but to receive awards! And from whom? The American Legion? The United Daughters of the Confederacy? "No—from *college students!*"

It was indeed hard to believe. A theater full of students, well into the second half of the twentieth century, standing in opposition to the overwhelming majority of their professors, Stakhanovite liberals. The straw poll at Yale registered two (2) faculty members favoring Goldwater for President. Two out of sixteen hundred. The academy had been suffering for two decades under the weight of intensive indoctrination in state welfarism, anti-anti-Communism, moral libertinage, skepticism, anti-Americanism. And here were these students foregathered, at the Herbst Theatre in San Francisco—the same building where delegates had met twenty years before to found the United Nations! And this was, arguably, the largest student assembly of the year, certainly the most enthusiastic, gathered to pay tribute, one after the other, to the most conspicuous symbols of everything they had studiously been taught by the intelligentsia to look down upon with contempt. It was as though the student body of the Lenin Institute had taken time off in the middle of the semester to pay tribute to the memory of the czar.

Five thousand persons were turned away. The auditorium was jammed with excited people, mostly under thirty years of age. The press was there in force. The professionalism of the physical arrangements was impressive. Marvin pointed out details Harvey might have missed . . . The hall was bedecked in color. Students from neighboring universities bore placards designating the college they represented. Large posters bearing pictures of Goldwater bobbed up and down, giving the floor the air of the convention hall seven miles away. The student band was first-rate. Flyers announcing the meeting were exuberantly laid out. The programs were well designed. The tickets were in three colors. Everything was done expressively, and well.

Brent Bozell and I had urged the YAF leaders to call public attention to the uniqueness of the event. Columnist George Sokolsky wrote a dispatch from the press room. "First, there had to be an animating spirit, as Bozell said. And that, of course, is Barry Goldwater. Then there had to be a technician in the art of public protest. Not even the officers of Young Americans for Freedom, for all their energy and intelligence, could have put on such a show unaided. The guiding hand was Marvin Liebman's, a young(ish) man who has emerged in recent months as principal impresario and coordinator of successful conservative and anti-Communist organizations and demonstrations. (It was he who organized the anti-Khrushchev demonstrations in 1959, and serves as executive secretary of the Committee of One Million against the Admission of Red China to the United Nations.) Let those who think they can put together such a meeting as was held tonight by YAF in San Francisco not try to do it without expert aid. It is a sign of the maturity of the directors of YAF that they know they need such help."

Sokolsky, who was awarded the prize for journalism that evening, spoke movingly in his two-minute acceptance speech. There is history to be made by American youth devoted to conservative principles, he said; and he was certain, as of that moment, that it would be made. "The future is ours—the faraway future, after we outgrow the superstitions of socialism. It is the job of youth," he concluded, "to turn the clock forward."

The crowd waited anxiously for the candidate. Finally, as it neared 11 P.M., Senator Goldwater came in and met a ten-minute ovation with a smile that warmed a room already overheated. He said that, negative reports on the GOP convention notwithstanding, they would have victory in the November election.

Rockefeller, watching the YAF program intently on television, turned to George Hinman. "You know, George, I think Barry actually believes all that stuff."

"Maybe that's why he's going to win the nomination," Hinman said, without moving his eyes from the box.

"Senator Barry Goldwater," the page-one story in the *New York Times* began the next day, "told a cheering stomping audience last night that the country was caught up in a wave of conservatism that could easily become the political phenomenon of our time."

18

"Extremism in the Defense of Liberty"

Goldwater's victory in California had communicated one thing to his supporters: that he would almost surely be nominated. His opponents were GOP leaders, but they did not make up an armed force. Henry Cabot Lodge resigned his post as ambassador to South Vietnam to look cautiously into the question of whom he might collude with to frustrate Goldwater. George Romney was no longer a central figure, but he was a voice in the GOP, and that voice rang out saying that the party could not win a national election with Goldwater as its head. General Eisenhower released his fifth ambiguity on the subject: Clearly he opposed Goldwater's nomination, and clearly he did not want to say so on the record. Ike was an organization man, and respect was paid to his preachments, which were seldom writ large and unmistakable, and had not been in the matter of Goldwater.

Still, William Scranton was there at the San Francisco convention, and he felt an afflatus on the question of Goldwater for President. He had been for several years, when he was governor of Pennsylvania, a member of the Republican high command, on companionable terms with other members of the GOP elect. Scranton had several times welcomed Goldwater to Pennsylvania to assist him in money-raising lunches and dinners. In December, Scranton had gone so far as to urge Goldwater to declare as a candidate. But it had to be, given Scranton's own political views, that in doing so he had assumed that exposure in a few primaries would deflate Goldwater and his movement. Goldwater amused himself, after the virulent anti-Goldwater turn Scranton took in San Francisco, by reflecting that it was Scranton who was substantially responsible for Goldwater's entry into the field. "Governor Scranton's persuasiveness is one of the major reasons I announced my own candidacy for the presidency."

One act of some desperation was done by (or for) Scranton at the convention. This was a letter hand-delivered to Goldwater's suite at the Mark Hopkins Hotel the evening before the convention began. It was a vicious attack on Goldwater and everything he stood for. Goldwater was understandably furious, but when he cooled down he and his advisors decided the most effective way of dealing with it was to distribute a copy of it under the door of every single delegate along with a note from Denison Kitchel quoting Abraham Lincoln's reply to an attack by Horace Greeley: "If there be perceptible in [this editorial] an impatient and dictatorial tone, I waive it in deference to an old friend, whose heart I have always supposed to be right."

Journalism, and history, designated the letter the "Scranton letter" for the soundest of reasons: The letter was signed, "William Scranton." The copies had been slid under the doors even before the morning papers were distributed. And the explosion was immediate. The tremor reached Governor Scranton, and by midmorning he had denied his authorship of the "Scranton letter."

The letter said that Senator Goldwater had treated delegates as "little more than a flock of chickens whose necks will be wrung at will." That the Goldwater delegates were "radical extremists" who were countenancing "irresponsibility in the serious question of racial holocaust."

For all of this, Scranton blamed two overeager aides. But of course the sentiments expressed in the letter were no more than tough crystallizations of the anti-Goldwater Weltanschauung. Goldwater should not be nominated because (1) he can't win, (2) he doesn't deserve to win, (3) America has most to fear a nuclear war, toward which (4) Goldwater's policies would head us, an enfeebled country given (5) his disdain for progressive social features of the past thirty years, including Social Security.

There was huge resentment of the Scranton letter among delegates who had worked for Goldwater and were exultant over what he might accomplish for his country if elected. But it was not easy for the delegates to express their resentment of the Scranton maneuver, whoever exactly was responsible for it. Goldwater (wisely) declined to answer Scranton in kind. He followed his practice of remaining in his hotel suite, though he did sneak out one morning, through a secret tunnel, and made his way to an airstrip at which a friend had put an airplane at his disposal, to shake off, so to speak, the dust of the convention.

What the delegates did to counter the anti-Goldwater sentiment was to express their partisanship on the convention floor. When Goldwater appeared on the floor to discharge a clerical requirement that he register, he received no less than a 42-second ovation.

But an embarrassing demonstration came on Day Three, when Nelson Rockefeller's turn came to address the convention. Anything he said that was remotely understandable as approval of Goldwater or Goldwater's doctrines brought great waves of applause and the whistling of assent. And when Rockefeller mentioned the name of a politician thought to be in the opposition, or even to be allied with the opposition, the house went crazy with scorn and derision. Rockefeller warned about "a radical, well-financed minority" that was "alien to the broad middle course that accommodates the mainstream of Republican principles," and the Cow Palace exploded with booing.

Given Clifton White's acknowledged brilliance in handling delegates, arrangements at the Cow Palace had been left in his hands. He proceeded to lay out the most intricate, comprehensive communications system in the history of technology. He could be put through to all the delegates, to any single delegate, to Goldwater, to the master of ceremonies. He could flash on his speaker and send out the words, "Cut it!" This had always worked for him before, permitting him to modulate public expressions of the delegates he controlled. But this time the roars and whistles continued, embarrassing Rockefeller, the principal figure identified with the opposition. But it was embarrassing also to White's effort to maintain decorum, a virile decorum, to be sure, but one that promised shelter to those who spoke out of turn while toning down the sound of applause enough to permit the scheduled proceedings to go forward.

A suspicion crossed the mind of Clif White, and of one or two other key members of the Goldwater team, that perhaps the unregulated booing was issuing from the spectator galleries—there, indeed, was where the noisiest demonstrations were coming from. But what to do about it, if indeed tickets had been handed out to hundreds who intended to cause consternation at the Goldwater convention?

It gradually, and then abruptly, transpired that the convention was driven by two passions. The first, now finally consolidated in Goldwater's victory, was resentment and hatred of the impotence of American foreign policy, the failure to respond to belligerent and continuing Soviet challenges with skill and daring and bravado. U.S.—and allied—strategy was scorned as ineffective, and inadequate in its expression of contempt for the Gulags of Communist life.

Angry and impatient Republicans could make out another great Soviet thrust in the making—in Indochina. Where were the guiding lights of an illuminated Republican policy? The thinking about the nature of the ongoing challenge had been done clearly by Goldwater. *Conscience* declared:

> I hesitate to restate the obvious—to say again what has been said so many times before by so many others: that the Communists' aim is to conquer the world. I repeat it because it is the beginning and the end of our knowledge about the conflict between East and West. I repeat it because I fear that however often we have given lip service to this central political fact of our time, very few of us have *believed* it. If we had, our entire approach to foreign policy over the past fourteen years would have been radically different, and the course of world events radically changed.

And then the second discontent, a palpable dissatisfaction with the "moderate" middle-of-the-road Republicanism that had ruled in domestic matters during the Eisenhower presidency. Dissenters at the convention needed to be discreet. Eisenhower was a Republican saint, and saints are beyond criticism.

Still, those dissenters felt that Ike had been historically overly submissive to what he accepted as the Zeitgeist: the collectivist approach to all social problems. To looking after health needs. To providing for workers' retirement. To financing education.

The turn will come when we entrust the conduct of our affairs to men who understand that their first duty as public officials is to divest themselves of the power they have been given. It will come when Americans, in hundreds of communities throughout the nation, decide to put the man in office who has pledged to enforce the Constitution and restore the Republic. Who will proclaim in a campaign speech: "I have little interest in streamlining government or in making it more efficient, for I mean to reduce its size. I do not undertake to promote welfare, for I propose to extend freedom. My aim is not to pass laws but to repeal them."

The attraction to Barry Goldwater was to someone who would not bend with the spirit of the age as president, any more than he had as legislator and political theorist. Perhaps he couldn't, at the Cow Palace, use the exact language he had written in his book. That much could not realistically be expected. But he could show that he was guided by policy recommendations that harmonized with the articles of faith explored in *The Conscience of a Conservative.* He had emerged, in San Francisco, as a true individualist, an outsider—a non-union man.

Early in the convention, opponents of Barry Goldwater felt the intensity of the inchoate challenge to Republican establishmentarianism. But for the most part, the regulars—the Rockefellers, the Scrantons, the Lodges—guarded their language. As did Goldwater, most of the time. (Informally, he could be scathing in his criticism.)

Although the spirit of defiance was not fully aroused in Goldwater in the days leading to his nomination, the spirit was alive in his mind, and it was bursting for air. He was careful not to appear like a Randian superego, strutting his individualism by scaling local skyscrapers. In San Francisco Barry appeared, mostly, as a compliant organization man in Sunday dress, the tiger properly dormant.

He sat there on the seventeenth floor of the Mark Hopkins Hotel in the company of his truly close associates. There were denunciations of Goldwater and his doctrines every day by disaffected delegates and, of course, by the press. Most of this only simmered outside the Mark Hopkins suite, but finally the criticism came within earshot, notwithstanding protective shielding by GOP regulars who simply wanted to get on with the business at hand—to nominate a presidential candidate. And then go home.

What on earth, Barry mused, had he ever said to justify the charge by California Governor Pat Brown that, with Goldwater, "The stench of fascism is in the air"? William Fulbright—Bill Fulbright, his learned colleague in the Senate!—said that Goldwaterism was "the closest thing in American politics to an equivalent of Russian Stalinism." The current issue of *Time* magazine quoted a Munich banker. "If we give you [Goldwaterites] four or five years, you'll start putting on brown shirts."

He never felt, in his bones, absolutely certain that he would be nominated. But he was orderly enough to commission the drafting of an acceptance speech. As his nomination neared, the intensity of the opposition heightened. Goldwater's bitterness hardened as he felt the force of the hostile camp—Eisenhower, Nixon, Rockefeller, Scranton, all of them, he knew or suspected, feeding a hostile press.

He had been briefly exhilarated by the delegates' response to the sentence in the speech by ex-President Dwight Eisenhower counseling against "sensation-seeking columnists and commentators," men and women "who couldn't care less about the good of our party." There had been cheers of joy to greet those words. But the diapasonal opposition drowned out the good moments, and Goldwater's appetite increased for a scorching comeback. He looked hungrily for an opportunity to go the whole hog—an expression of contempt for and defiance of the critics. By Thursday night, he had found the means to do this. In a single passage. One passage in his acceptance speech, in which he fired out the most notorious rhetorical couplet in modern political history.

At the end of his final meeting with his speechwriters, the manuscript (hotly sought after by the delegates, by the press, and by his own staff—only four of them had yet seen it) was escorted to two secretaries in a hotel room without telephones, a Goldwater agent standing guard against interception.

There was no difficulty in justifying his formulations intellectually. Morally, they expressed sentiments universally accepted. Ceremonially, they reflected the exalted ambitions of a pedigreed political party, out of power but seeking reinstatement. The actual wording had been suggested by Professor Harry Jaffa of Claremont McKenna College, a learned political theorist who consistently, in his teaching and writing, had placed human freedom as the first political priority. Researchers soon discovered that the explosive sentiments, mutatis mutandis, could be found easily in the oratory of exhortation.

I would remind you that extremism in the defense of liberty is no vice. And let me remind you also that moderation in the pursuit of justice is no virtue.

A routine rhetorical device, the vitalizing contrast of images. (*Live by the sword, perish by the sword.*) John F. Kennedy, in his inaugural address, had exhorted the citizenry to ask not what their country could do for them, but to ask what they could do for their country. *National Review* asked its readers to identify the source of three quotations: "Justice too long delayed is justice denied"; "There comes a time when the cup of endurance runs over, and men are no longer willing to be plunged into an abyss of injustice when they experience the blackness of corroding despair"; and, "I have been greatly disappointed by the moderates."

All three phrases had been used by the Reverend Martin Luther King Jr.

Ah, but Goldwater was not Martin Luther King Jr.

So general and so adamant were the protests against what was taken as a license granted by Republican extremists to the Ku Klux Klan and the John Birch Society that General Eisenhower, shaken, summoned Goldwater to his hotel suite for an explanation satisfactory to himself and to his brother Milton, president of Johns Hopkins University, who was standing by.

Goldwater ended the discussion by commenting that the troops General Eisenhower had led across the channel in 1944 could only be described as having taken an extremist position on how to defeat Hitler, and that satisfied Ike.

Fifteen years later, when Ronald Reagan was preparing to declare for the presidency, a friend (it was I) said to him, in the playful way that always appealed to Reagan, that he should not permit himself even to pronounce the word "nuclear" other than in a phrase denouncing or warning against nuclear weapons.

Reagan was amused, but also informed. Goldwater had learned too late the lesson that one must guard against any use of a word which, for many, amounted to a call to immoral ends (for decades, the word "condom" carried the taboo). He guilelessly discussed the possibility of using low-grade *nuclear* weapons to eliminate the forests along the

Ho Chi Minh Trail, under the cover of which the North Vietnamese were carrying on their bloody war against the south. There was hell to pay.

It was so in 1964 with the word "extremism." It could not be hygienically used in any affirmative context.

19

The Ghost of JFK

Goldwater had been nominated in July, President Johnson renominated in August. In Atlantic City for the Democratic convention, LBJ had generated suspense by his apparent indecision as to whom he would name for vice president. Finally he resolved on the favorite, Hubert Humphrey. Humphrey came on stage to a roar of approval.

Johnson had a capacity for acidulous commentary, and the theatrical lights pulsated, awaiting a show of his skills at the expense of his sometime Senate colleague, GOP challenger Barry Goldwater. But Johnson's mockery did not come. Everyone expected that before leaving Atlantic City he would find an opportunity to mangle Goldwater as best he could. But he did only humdrum duty, accepting the nomination.

He began his campaign in New England, stressing and restressing his memory of his glowing predecessor, John F. Kennedy. His remarks invoking the memory of the martyred president drew teeming and grateful crowds—100,000 adoring fans in Portland, 250,000 in Hartford, a record-setting 500,000 in Providence. He had decided on the theme that would sustain him throughout the presidential campaign. At a news conference in Gettysburg a week later, ex-President Eisenhower commented on the strange phenomenon. "This campaign is more personal than any I have ever known," said Ike. "The candidates are just not debating, not debating the issues."

Once or twice, in the weeks ahead, Johnson let out a little partisan obbligato, as when he ran the television ad of the little girl with the daisy overwhelmed by a nuclear bomb—dispatched, the viewer was encouraged to suppose, by President Goldwater's extremism.

And Goldwater? He too was unusually quiet.

It was not as if the election contest was ignored. In a single week, LBJ gave nearly two dozen speeches, traveled 2,900 miles, gave three press conferences, appeared three times on national television. He shook hands so profligately he was said to be bleeding from this exercise in brotherhood.

Frank Meyer was in New York in September for *National Review*'s fortnightly editorial dinner. In the conference room, after the editorial copy had finally been surrendered to the messenger, he gave vent to his disconsolation. Frank was truly satisfied only when engaged in combat. It was a kind of physical exercise for him, the neglect of which gnawed at his convivial good humor, mostly exhibited after he had scored against the enemy. The enemy today was, no less, Barry Goldwater. "Why doesn't he *say* something!"

Burnham's strength, always the philosopher, was his concern for underlying meaning. "Frank, Goldwater hasn't denied any of the principles we expound at *National Review*. But the political situation binds him in ways we need to understand. If you were the candidate I know you'd indulge the joy of fighting like an alley cat—"

"Which is why you aren't the candidate," I said. "But I know what you're saying, Frank. We aren't going to win, so why not walk off with certain—"

"Satisfactions." Priscilla obliged, as usual, with just the right word.

Frank Meyer was not so easily appeased. "Do you suppose, Brent, that our candidate forbids his speechwriters to read *The Conscience of a Conservative?*"

The turning of eyes toward Brent reminded him how any mention of the book, which was now in its seventeenth printing, was so easily taken as an invitation to honor it—or to regret its existence.

Burnham could manage to do both: He enjoyed quintessential political prose, of the kind Bozell had used. But Burnham the political operative deplored work at cross-purposes. It was one thing for *National Review*, a combative conservative journal, to stress the paradigm, another to insist that to do so was sensible for a candidate for high political office. "Frank, you probably would be happy to have Goldwater lose a million votes every week, as long as he deplored free milk."

"If he deplored free milk he might introduce political reality."

"Frank, political *reality* is what *Conscience* is not talking about. That essay is about devising rules for a virginal political state based on libertarian extrapolations . . ."

"What do you think, Jim, the Declaration of Independence was, if not a sequence of libertarian extrapolations?"

"The Declaration of Independence," Burnham retorted, "was an incitement. To ultimate affirmations—to treason, to—"

"Extremism?" I volunteered. "Which reminds me, Frank, if you light one more cigarette in this room, I will forget about my reputation for conciliation and discretion, and tell the police that the late Frank Meyer was still a secret member of the Communist Party, bent on disrupting the Goldwater campaign."

Frank liked that. He liked to be reminded of having been a Communist. "If you were once a Communist and left the party, then you have achieved something in your life. It's a heroic testimonial of sorts."

"Why," Rusher asked, "don't you rejoin the party, then resign from it again? Wouldn't that make you doubly heroic?"

It was time to go to dinner.

"I need a drink," Frank said.

"What about those who've listened to you? What do we need?" Bozell asked his closest friend.

20

Heading Home

Barry Goldwater was at the controls of his Boeing 727, hired for the duration of his campaign. He was never without an airplane, but he hadn't had so large a plane at his disposal since the Second World War. Back then, Goldwater had had to fly it wherever the high command told him to go.

"*I* am the high command in this show," he ruminated, easing the rudder a little left and, twenty seconds later, a little right, a routine airborne exercise, supplementary precautions to guard against mid-air collisions. These were pretty unlikely, given the strict rules about altitude maintenance on different flight azimuths. Even so, about ten minutes further on, on this azimuth, he would be able to look down, assuming there was still enough daylight, on the surviving remains of the United airplane that, eight years ago, ran into a TWA airplane in mid-morning above the Grand Canyon. He had growled at Barry Jr. when he came to breakfast the next day chanting, *Fly United and meet your friends at TWA.* "Okay, so kids will be kids, but not in my house, not about fatal air accidents."

Yes, he was king of his own show and he could do what he wanted to do. He was supposed to want, above all things, victory at the polls next Tuesday. Karl Hess had told him about a psychological paper revealing, or in any event presuming to reveal, that every candidate in the history of elections has believed at some point that he is going to win.

"Bullshit."

For him to beat Lyndon Johnson, they'd have to publish pictures of LBJ having at it with his homosexual aide, Walter Jenkins. Goldwater was pleased with himself that, to the near-mutinous chagrin of his aides, he had absolutely forbidden the staff to exploit the Jenkins disclosure, male-sex-at-the-YMCA.

"Don't you understand, Barry, this election is about morality in government—"

Goldwater understood. He understood basic things very quickly. "Jenkins has a wife and six children. Leave him alone."

He did resent it when he learned later that Abe Fortas and Clark Clifford, the two top legal honchos in the Democratic establishment, had actually called on the publishers of the three top newspapers in Washington urging them not to run the story. It almost worked, but of course, some reporter got hold of it, and then it became national news for days.

But not with any help from me.

Barry stole a glance at the instruments. *All's well.*

And since he was ruler of his own roost, king of his skies, head of the second-largest political party in America, why did he let them treat him as a puppet? *Go here, puppet. Go there.* Barry Goldwater was not thought of as a verbal man. But that was entirely mistaken. He read books and he wrote books and he wrote letters and he scribbled notes.

He had taken pains, at the end of the previous Thursday, to list that day's activities . . . At 2 A.M. he went over the next day's schedule with Denny Kitchel. After sleeping for three hours, he went from the 7 A.M. television interview to an 8 A.M. breakfast and speech to a 9 A.M. outdoor rally and speech in downtown Billings, Montana. Then to a 10 A.M. flight to Cheyenne, Wyoming, with a noon rally and speech on the grounds of the state Capitol, then a 12:30 lunch with leading townsfolk, followed by a news conference. Then he took off for Denver at 1:30 for an airport rally and news conference there before heading to Albuquerque for a 4 P.M. news conference, a 6 P.M. dinner speech, and an outdoor speech at the University of New Mexico at 8 P.M. A strategy session with the gang—the Arizona Mafia, as they called themselves—was scheduled for 9 P.M., including discussions of financing, advertising, and speechwriting. He told Kitchel, "You guys are killing me." So he had told him a few dozen times.

The trouble had come on those few occasions when he made up his mind to flat-out say NO.

So—when that happened—which event would he amputate? And how to handle the crestfallen aide whose championship of that single eight-minute stop he would *predictably* announce was the crowning accomplishment of his life as campaign worker?

It wasn't that LBJ had it all that easy. But there is a difference when it's the president who is doing it. For one thing, nobody complains that you're late. That would be *swell*—Barry allowed himself to think he had become president. For presidents, the schedule plays for you, not the other way around. And you can get away with a lot.

He took his folder from the co-pilot's lap and plucked out the clipping on LBJ's visit to Phoenix—*my Phoenix!*—last Sunday. It had been written by John Kolbe—Barry knew John Kolbe, who had been a *Gazette* reporter for years.

Kolbe's story recorded that the President "made nineteen speeches on the way from the airport to the church, arriving two hours later." The minister was standing in front of the church; the congregation was "waiting inside."

"The President," Kolbe had written, "drew to a stop in the presidential limousine. He yelled through a bullhorn at the crowd: 'Sorry, I've got to go now, folks, I'm late for church.'"

Goldwater stared at the clipping. *If I'd done that, they'd have killed me. Good independent men and women of Arizona. It takes a president—no, it takes a president called Lyndon Baines Johnson—to emasculate the proud people of Arizona. Shee-yit.*

But now he could make out the lights of his beloved Phoenix, welcoming him home.

21

The Eve of Disaster

Goldwater, though sociable by disposition, did not invite a gang to his house for election evening. There was such a party, but it was held at the Camelback Inn. To his home, Goldwater beckoned only his family, plus Denison Kitchel, Karl Hess, and Governor Paul Fannin. These three insiders abided by the same rules that govern in social situations when a member of the royal family is present: You say nothing about national affairs unless He, or She, raises the subject.

Barry didn't talk about the election. But he was not going to be without his workaday emollient, and he had several shots of Old Crow before informing the group, at about 11 P.M., that—he was going to bed.

"You've got a problem, Barry, just fading away," Fannin objected. "It's not right to fail to congratulate the winner."

"The winner, Paul, has not been announced."

That, actually, was true. All three networks had called the election already, granted, but it was not yet official. The

California polls had not closed until 8 P.M.—not that the California vote could have done anything to reverse the massive returns flooding in. Which read, simply: Lyndon Johnson. By a landslide.

But Goldwater also had a formal excuse for not sitting up any longer—LBJ had not yet issued a victory statement.

"It doesn't work that way," Fannin stopped him. "The loser concedes first, and then the winner takes his bow."

"I don't think that makes sense," said Barry. "The winner crosses the line—he goes to the victory circle and says all those things."

Fannin didn't want to argue any more, and Peggy said nothing. It was just as well.

Goldwater's mind was crowded with the paradoxes of it all. He would lose to Johnson 2 to 1, or nearly so. He had sensed this for some weeks now. None of the little shafts of optimistic unreason by volunteers and idolators affected his judgment in the least, though he was always careful to express, with a smile, gladness over sanguine data brought in by fans as if they had just flown in from Dr. Gallup's laboratory.

But there were paradoxes he could not understand, and which he found arresting. A recent Harris Poll revealed that no less than 94 percent of the American public believed that the government had been lax in security. (But this was largely a reflection of the Walter Jenkins episode—the confidant of a president keeping sex dates with stray men just blocks from the Oval Office. Shouldn't security have got onto that sooner?) And apparently 88 percent agreed that prayer in schools should be reinstated. This was a contention on which LBJ had stood aside, with occasional loving thoughts expressed for the Supreme Court, together with tributes to the constitutional separation of powers. How did that son of a bitch get away with it?

Sixty-four percent believed that Goldwater was uniquely serious about wanting to curb extremist groups; 60 percent felt that government power should be trimmed; and, again, 60 percent agreed that state welfare without stringent eligibility rules encouraged laziness. A solid 50 percent believed that Goldwater would do a better job than Johnson on the issue of morality and corruption in government.

Would the lopsided vote today undermine those figures?

He didn't think so, but the last thing he felt like doing now was to raise those fundamental questions. What he wanted now was to go to bed. He dreaded the possibility that any of the people gathered in this house—his favorite people, his family and political partners—would be so gross as to say to him, as he turned to the staircase, that by the time he woke up, a great and favorable reversal would have overtaken the current news. If anybody said that, including Peggy, he would pour his drink over their head.

But not so fast. He wanted to take that drink upstairs, to his bedside. Messrs. Gallup and Harris, ABC, CBS, NBC, and the fucking *New York Times* could not take that glass away from him, whatever the voters decided in Colorado.

And Arizona?

Who knows. Maybe I'll lose Arizona! Those dumb sons of bitches, maybe Peggy and I should consider moving.

To where?

To my bedroom!

He nodded and waved once again with his spare hand, mounting the stairs. He wasn't seen again until 6 A.M., his regular hour for rising. He put on a bathrobe, intending to walk over to his carpentry shop, next to his radio shed, and resume work he had neglected on the assembly of a color television set he had promised his secretary, Judy Eisenhower.

But whoa! Peggy, in her pajamas, accosted him. And with good reason. He had to send "a message" to President Johnson. "There are forty people outside, been waiting for you all night."

"What was the vote?"

"Sixty-one to 39."

"Arizona?"

"You took Arizona. You also took Mississippi, Alabama, Louisiana, South Carolina—"

"And Georgia?"

"Yes, and Georgia. Now, Barry, Judy's on call in the guest room. She'll take your dictation and write it up for the press. And Barry?"

"Yes?"

"Be nice."

"All right, dear."

22

Reagan: A Fresh Star

He wondered whether he should send a special message to Ronald Reagan. That had been a sudden and mixed-up affair, the Reagan speech. It had come toward the end of the campaign. He remembered the date, October 27. He wondered yet again how it could have been that Baroody and Kitchel had *opposed* its release. Goldwater winced at ascribing bad motives for such obtuse conduct, but he could not avoid reading what was there in the press during the campaign. About the Reagan broadcast and how so much had been done by Goldwater's own staff to prevent its airing.

Their actions were, in the end, explainable, even if not commendable. To begin with, the Reagan speech was not Goldwater's property, not even the property of the campaign. It had been an adaptation of a speech Reagan had given to a business group in Los Angeles. That speech hugely impressed conservative Goldwater backers, most especially

Walter Knott, the wealthy founder of Knott's Berry Farm and chairman of the Goldwater TV committee.

Reagan had recorded the talk fresh, before a live audience, and it was received with huge enthusiasm by Knott and other backers eager to give it nationwide exposure. But a deflationary word came: on the advice of William Baroody in particular, the Arizona Mafia had ruled against associating Goldwater with Reagan's talk. Instead of airing it, Baroody had suggested, why not stick into that half-hour of reserved network time a rerun of Goldwater's tête-à-tête with Eisenhower? Or maybe rerun the half-hour titled "Brunch with Barry"?

Goldwater called Reagan, suggesting the substitute program. Reagan replied that any alternative use of the half-hour would need to be okayed by the Knott group, which had reserved and paid for the time. Reagan asked Goldwater if he had any specific objections to the speech. Goldwater replied that, as a matter of fact, he had never viewed it. But he said he would arrange to do this quickly. Two days later he did so and turned in astonishment to Baroody. "What the hell's wrong with *that*?" He immediately phoned Reagan and told him as much.

Still Baroody objected—encouraged, some said, by the advertising agency that had the Goldwater account. Since they hadn't handled the Reagan speech, they would forfeit advertising commissions if it rather than something they had handled ran in that time slot.

The indecision was rapidly cleared up by Walter Knott. It was the work of a single telephone call. He told Kitchel that if the Reagan speech was not aired, he—Knott—would pull out the money he had set aside for the half-hour and return it to the donors.

And so Reagan's speech was aired.

Dwight Eisenhower had viewed it from his hospital bed at Walter Reed, where he was undergoing routine tests, and pronounced it "the best thing" he had seen in the campaign. Columnists David Broder and Stephen Hess called the speech "the most successful national political debut since William Jennings Bryan electrified the 1896 Democratic convention." It generated over a half million dollars in contributions to the Goldwater campaign.

It occurred to a few sibylline viewers that they were on to a new and very bright political star. Reagan had accomplished, even if unintentionally, much more than a last-minute boost for Goldwater's campaign. He had set in motion a movement of Californians who would send him to the statehouse in Sacramento, and, of course—though no one could see that far at the time—on to the White House.

The acclaim given the speech was heartier than was welcomed by some loyal Goldwater staffers. And Barry, though he paid tribute to the speech in later years, did not express himself so generously on it at the time it was aired. This indifference offended Nancy Reagan, always easily offended by any slight, actual or hypothetical, against her husband.

She mentioned to a biographer that Goldwater had never properly thanked Reagan for the speech.

There was the making of bad blood there, and a rupture of sorts would open in 1976. Reagan was in Kansas City for the Republican convention, competing against the nomination of Gerald Ford, the incumbent president. Rejecting the Reagan candidacy, Senator Goldwater stuck by President Ford. In doing so, he assured that the Goldwaters would not be invited to the White House during the eight golden years of President Reagan that lay ahead.

23

The Vision of Karl Hess

Karl Hess had a gift for sensing when his presence was wanted, as also a gift for not speaking when his host simply didn't want conversation. Those qualities made most people welcome his company. Having spent the whole of election day at the side of Goldwater, finally, after midnight, he left the house and drove back to his room at the Camelback Inn. He slept a tormented sleep. Waking early he wondered what to do. If governed by instinct, he would climb into his rented car and drive to Be-Nun-I-Kin and reinsinuate himself into Goldwater's life.

He closed his eyes and let his imagination go to work. If he presented himself there he would be moved into the same room in the main house that, for the campaign, had been converted into a study in which four aides could work. Or . . . At Goldwater's house Karl Hess could do anything he liked. Peggy and Felipa would not be surprised to see him anywhere, and it would never occur to them that he was imposing on the household of the man Felipa always called, pure and simple, "El Señor."

But Hess didn't stir from his hotel room. Somehow things were different now, made so just overnight. Things would never again be as they had been for over a year, when he had been at the side of Barry Goldwater day after day, staying up to compose speeches for him, trading tales about Johnson, or his aides, or his aides' aides, and eventually, even about Goldwater's own people. There was nothing Goldwater had hesitated to talk about with Karl Hess. Yet it had all depended on that vital, sustaining background: the historic race for a hugely important public office, with everything Barry said putting a claim of sorts on history—because Candidate Goldwater said it, even if it was Karl Hess who had written it.

Karl was only forty-one, but a confirmed vagrant, back to when, at age fifteen, he left school, and set out to find work. He did so as a news writer for a company that had offices in the same building where his mother worked as a telephone operator. He was professionally adept, and quickly found a job with the *Washington Daily News* and later as a press editor for *Newsweek*.

It was then, in the company of *Newsweek*'s Ralph de Toledano, that he took to meeting regularly with me, and the three of us plotted together the rescue of the world—which would be done in part through my new magazine, *National Review*, which Hess did what he could to bring to life.

Hess lived in a small but cozy house near Mount Vernon with a wife and child, both of whom he seemed to cherish deeply, as he cherished also his religious faith—Karl was a Catholic, and in his zany way he would sometimes explain that the world's problems had begun with the dissolution of the Holy Roman Empire.

Then he all but disappeared. He left his job, wife, religion, and, briefly, his son. A few years later he had joined forces with Goldwater and was always at his side, composing striking sentences for his chief.

The line about extremism Karl Hess took very much to heart. After the polls closed it was instantly clear to him that he would need to make his own way—to face, once again, the extremism of life outside the Goldwater retinue, which now would all but evaporate.

Goldwater had no more contributors' money coming in. And he had given up his own job as senator. In that bleak period he retained on his staff only his secretary, Judy Eisenhower. He renewed his contract with his lecture agent.

He had had a final dinner with Karl, and listened to Karl's personal story, never before revealed. Goldwater did not comment on Karl's intellectual journey, now disclosed to him. He just listened. Karl Hess was edging, with excitement almost spiritual in nature, toward a political philosophy that came close to anarchy.

Well, such things happen, Goldwater told himself, though a historical parallel did not come to mind. But he forced himself to listen to a fairly elaborate philosophical analysis by his dear friend and principal speechwriter.

Karl's thesis was that Goldwater's electoral loss was owing not to his unyielding opposition to liberal policies but rather to his failure to discover for himself another enchanted world and, upon discovering it, to inform the American public—abject from lack of sufficient thought given to the meaning of liberty—of the true opportunity that lay for them in the rejection of all government, all coercion.

Later, Barry reported to Peggy on the conversation. "Presumably," Peggy commented impatiently, "staying with his wife was something Karl thought coercive."

Barry changed the subject. He didn't want to disparage Karl. And he didn't want to enter into theoretical discussions about freedom from—everything.

In November 1968, Barry Goldwater was returned to the Senate. One day, threading his way through an antiwar protest in front of the Capitol, he spotted Karl Hess, and they had a warm public embrace. But soon after, Barry learned that Hess had abandoned journalism altogether. He had set up as a welder. He attracted publicity when attempting to sell a piece of sculpture while contending with the Internal Revenue Service, which had imposed a 100 percent lien on everything Hess earned, attempting to collect tax money owed.

Hess pursued his anarchical visions in books and other writings, and there was a posthumous autobiography, *Mostly on Edge*, edited by his son. Although they were no longer in touch, Barry never spoke an unkind word about his former speechwriter.

24

Eisenhower's Steely Analysis

Four years after he left the White House, Dwight Eisenhower continued to live, for the most part happily—he missed his habitual supremacy in all matters—on his property in Gettysburg. It had been a modest farmhouse, its original structure still discernible through the alterations made in it after Ike took it on. These were done in two stages, the first when he was still in the White House.

George Humphrey, the friendly tycoon who had been secretary of the treasury for Ike and had ancillary responsibility for presidential security, gave the building what he called a "light carapace." But after the assassination of President Kennedy, the Secret Service substantially revised what had been thought acceptable security accommodations, and the Gettysburg dwelling received what Humphrey might have described as a heavy carapace. Now all the walls were bulletproofed, and fire alarms and smoke detectors were multiplied. "We're talking, after all," incumbent Treasury Secretary Douglas Dillon told his staff, "about one of only three living ex-presidents." The two officers guarding the entrance were buttressed by a third officer posted on the 230-acre property with his radio, alert to any irregularities.

General Eisenhower was accustomed to a life of command structures. He had had one of sorts when serving, however briefly, as president of Columbia University, and of course at the White House. And even in retirement there was a miniature representation of it. Lieutenant Colonel Harry McKay was there as chief of staff. Straight-backed and firm in all matters, he had his private office, a secretary, and, when he chose to use it, an on-premise bedroom. Ida Turnbull ran the office within, with three assistants. Mostly, they answered mail, trivial and non-trivial: Historians were always seeking more information from, and about, the thirty-fourth president of the United States.

Ida placed about a dozen selected letters on the general's desk every day. In the last four months she had increased the ration substantially because it seemed that everybody the president had ever known, and many men and women who had never met him but who respected him as the fons et origo of American political wisdom, had taken to writing him about . . . Barry Goldwater, nominated by the Republican Party to be the next successor to Dwight Eisenhower at the White House. "Assuming it's even conceivable," he remarked to Harry McKay at their regular 11 o'clock conference, "that anyone can edge Lyndon outta there."

Harry nodded. Yes, he was agreeing, that would take some doing.

"It will take more doing than Barry Goldwater's got, I'm afraid."

McKay passed along a folder of letters from people abroad. Some of them had known Eisenhower, either when he was supreme commander of the military force that concluded the war, or after that, when he served as supreme commander of NATO. After the convention at San Francisco, queries were very numerous, many of them anxious. Eisenhower wrote out a form note for use in replying to such letters, which he would close with a personal word or two.

The standard note read: "The Republican nominee, Barry Goldwater, is a gentleman of much experience, and is devoted to ideals he and I have in common. He is more emphatic than I have been in wishing to restore some Republican traditions, but none of these would damage any goal you and I share."

After election day, he told McKay he did not want to discuss what had happened with any member of the press, beyond giving out copies of the conventional congratulations he had sent to President Johnson. He wished, he told McKay, to confer personally only with his brother Milton, with George Humphrey, and with Lucius Clay, former governor of the conquered Germany, and close advisor to the former president.

His guests arrived at Gettysburg with their drivers before noon on Thursday, in time for a light lunch. Eisenhower wanted to start in immediately on the matter at hand. "Milton," he began, "has collected some statements from our least-favorite journalists."

"Yes," said Milton Eisenhower, president of Johns Hopkins University. "But it wasn't they who lost the vote on Tuesday, Ike."

The two others addressed Eisenhower as "General." He had told them he preferred this to "Mr. President." "I was president, but I'll always be a general." He nodded to Milton to proceed.

"Well here is Scotty Reston, king at the *New York Times*, and pretty much king of American opinion."

"I wouldn't put it that way, Milton. I mean, he's not king of *my* opinion."

"Okay, Ike. Anyway"—he picked up the folder he had brought in—"Reston wrote yesterday, 'Barry Goldwater not only lost the presidential election yesterday, but the conservative cause as well. He has wrecked his party for a long time to come and is not even likely to control the wreckage.'"

"That's bullshit, General," Humphrey interrupted. Eisenhower paused for a moment but then nodded to Milton to go on.

"Here is Tom Wicker, also for the *Times,* but a little more specific. He says, 'The Republicans strayed from the simple reality that they cannot win'—I'm quoting him exactly— 'cannot win in this era of American history except as a me-too party. With tragic inevitability, yesterday they cracked like a pane of glass.'"

Ike looked up, a half-smile showing. "Milton, you're the academic. First of all"—the brothers enjoyed their wisecracks—"did what happened give off the sound that cracked glass gives?"

Humphrey joined in the guffaws, but then consulted his own notes: "Thirty-six GOP congressmen who formally endorsed Goldwater were re-elected, and eighteen—yeah, eighteen—were defeated. But George Murphy took the Senate seat from Pierre Salinger in California. Yes, it was a helluva defeat, but I'm here to say that there is a difference between the defeat of Barry Goldwater and the defeat of the policies he spoke for."

Milton Eisenhower raised his hand. "Here's Walter Lippmann. He writes, 'The Johnson majority'—that was 61 percent, the greatest popular mandate in history—'is indisputable proof that the voters are in the center.'

"And we won't end the survey with Lippmann. Here's the *Los Angeles Times*: 'If the Republicans become a conservative party, advocating reactionary changes at home and adventures abroad that might lead to war, they will remain a minority party forever.'"

Milton went on. "These gentlemen, of course, are Democrats. But the critics aren't all Democrats. Here's the GOP chief in New York State—brace yourselves: 'The party has paid a shattering price for the erratic deviation from our soundly moderate twentieth-century course.'"

"Okay, okay," General Eisenhower said. "We can think about all that, especially after Congress resumes. Let me have copies of what you've read out," he addressed Milton and Humphrey. "And let's see what Mamie's done about chow."

He led the way into the dining room. He did say, after they had sat down, "If the Lord spares me for 1968, I'm going to come out at least eighteen months ahead of time. This year I tried to do what was decent."

"So did Goldwater, General," Clay said.

Eisenhower snapped back. "He needs a little practice, is all I can say."

25

Flying High

Brent Bozell and I were nowhere to be seen in the front lines of Barry Goldwater's campaign. We could guess the principal reason for this early on—the megalomania of Bill Baroody—but speculation ended after Goldwater's first autobiography, in 1979. Indeed William Baroody, on whom Barry relied, had passed the word down that the candidate should distance himself personally and professionally from "the *National Review* people."

That meant, concretely, Brent Bozell, the author of *The Conscience of a Conservative*, and me, the editor and founder of *National Review* and, as such, putative godfather of the conservative movement which Goldwater represented on the political front.

Goldwater had submitted to the sequestration—a matter of staff solidarity, it was plain. Mostly this was effected by little motions of inclusion and exclusion, which the candidate himself might well have been unaware of. But only

Goldwater could have been the instrument of exclusion when, in San Francisco during the convention, I went up to his seventeenth-floor suite to visit and found the candidate's manner, judged by historical experience, abrupt. And Goldwater himself must have acquiesced—if ever he was consulted in the matter—in the directive from his campaign headquarters that I was not to appear as a speaker at the much-touted Youth for Goldwater rally on the first day of the convention.

The dissociation did not affect the magazine's enthusiastic endorsement of Goldwater's candidacy. And in the many months of the Goldwater movement, pre–San Francisco, I and others at the magazine wrote corporately and severally about Goldwater. Most strikingly ignored was a special supplement to the magazine entitled, "A Program for a Goldwater Administration." Never has so much thought been given to a document so concentratedly ignored by the intended recipient. I go so far as to wonder, even at this remove, forty-three years later, whether Goldwater ever laid eyes on it, such was the thoroughness of the hands-on taboo of Baroody. It was inconceivable that Goldwater would not even have acknowledged these essays by James Burnham on foreign policy, James Jackson Kilpatrick on the domestic scene, and Colm Brogan and others on stray discontents.

Others noticed the vaporization at Goldwater headquarters of National Review, Inc., more keenly than I did. I tended, out of habit, to rely on the durability of friendships and on an organic unity among admirers of *The Conscience* of a *Conservative*, of *National Review*, and of the Clif White–Bill Rusher Suite 3505 activists for Goldwater's nomination.

One year after Goldwater's nomination, I gave my political attention to local challenges. Specifically, I objected to the absence of a political party in New York which endorsed the positions of the Right, and I accordingly declared my candidacy for mayor of New York City. This was a quixotic venture on the face of it, my political positions being pretty much those of *Conscience*, which assured my virtual isolation in big bad New York City, hotbed of American liberalism.

Yet it was there that the New York Conservative Party had been founded in 1962. Its importance was, at first, purely symbolic: Its first candidate for governor (in 1964) barely got the 100,000 signatures required to merit listing on the ballot. But while we acknowledged that my own campaign could not win the election, it could certainly serve to reform the state's Republican organization.

The campaign was not a genuine mountain-climbing of the kind essayed by Goldwater, but rather an exercise in political education. Yet I attracted considerable attention from the moment of my first press conference ("What would be the first thing you would do if you won?" "Demand a recount.") on through my disquisitional position papers on the problems that faced New York (poor education, crime, insolvency, the water shortage, etc., all of them reproduced in my book *The Unmaking of a Mayor*). There was substantial exegesis of conservative policies, including an analysis of the shortcomings of the Social Security law and of efforts to centralize medicine and education—all of this apart from the high jinks that figure in almost every political campaign.

My campaign manager was my older brother James Buckley, a calm and engaging presence who went on, astonishingly, to be elected U.S. senator from New York on the Conservative ticket in 1970.

It was Jim who thought it logical to solicit the explicit support of Barry Goldwater, even though, in the New York race we were entering, one contender was a regularly anointed GOP candidate, rising star John Lindsay. Goldwater had served twice as head of the Republican Senatorial Campaign Committee before his presidential race and had counseled severely on the need for party loyalty. How could he be expected, now, to break ranks with the GOP in New York by endorsing someone running on the Conservative Party ticket?

Even so, somehow it didn't surprise me when Goldwater, in a simple letter, authorized Jim to announce that I had the backing of Barry Goldwater in my race for mayor of New York on the Conservative Party ticket.

But I ruled against conveying the endorsement to the press. I reasoned that to associate Goldwater directly with my own (slightly idiosyncratic) political fortunes might suggest that the strength of conservative ranks in New

York would thenceforward be measured by my own show-ing in the 1965 contest. Goldwater, in 1964, was the offi-cial standard-bearer of the GOP, and had received eight hundred thousand votes in the boroughs of New York City. I judged it inconceivable that I, running as a third-party candidate, would do as well. I didn't want a vote far slen-derer than Goldwater's to confirm the judgment of politi-cal critics that there was waning popular acceptance of conservative policies.

So I acknowledged Goldwater's note, thanked him for the endorsement, and explained why I was not using it.

This would have, I reasonably deduced, the effect on Goldwater of acutely reminding him of the rebuff of me and *National Review* during his own campaign. A day or two later I had a telephone call from him. Could I and brother Jim—"and anyone else you'd like"—join him for lunch in New York?

What was he up to? my associates wondered. I replied that he was up to being a nice guy.

It worked out that he would ride with me in my station wagon from his hotel to my office, to pay a visit to my fel-low editors of *National Review*—he wanted, as he put it, to stop by and pay his respects, even though his old friend and backer Bill Rusher was out of town. I was at the wheel of the car, Goldwater seated alongside, my thirteen-year-old son, en route to school, in the back seat with his mother.

Christopher was wild with excitement at sharing a car ride with the Republican nominee of 1964.

Suddenly, from the back, the thirteen-year-old soprano voice was heard: "Senator, do you want to hear a joke?"

"Why sure, Christopher."

"Well, there was this Jew."

I thought fleetingly to abort the conversation by running my car up against the Park Avenue embankment. What might Christopher come out with! I held my breath.

"So?" Goldwater said pleasantly.

"Well," Christopher continued, "this Jew's son set fire to the house and then ran over his dad with the tractor, cutting off his leg. When the father got back from the hospital, he went to his yard and looked up at the clouds and said, 'God, what have I done to deserve this treatment from my own son?' And God appeared in the clouds and said to him, 'Well, at least yours didn't become a Catholic.'"

The contingent crisis was survived, we visited in the office, Goldwater made another ten lifelong friends, and we went on to lunch. It was very pleasant, genuinely affectionate.

"Maybe you should run for president again in 1968?" I said, in mock solemn tones.

"Maybe I will," Barry said. "But only if you and *National Review* promise to back me." I made the promise.

Coda

The years ahead were, by the standards of Barry Goldwater, unhurried. The master compiler, *Facts on File*, has only a handful of Goldwater entries per year after 1965. He had resigned his Senate seat in 1964, to conform to his own preachments on the subject of running simultaneously for separate political offices. What everyone knew was that he was, so to speak, out of school, taking a long vacation. And no one was surprised when in 1968 he announced his re-entry into public life, waking up on November 6, 1968, a freshman member of the Senate.

There were ideological questions, in political quarters, arising from the explosive Goldwater experience of 1964. The answers to those questions were not found in any meticulous exploration of either his words or his votes in his later years. He was accepted as a historical figure who had made the supreme bid for power, losing that bid but remaining a presence always to be coped with, whether crossing the aisle in the legislature, or appearing at the other end of the editorial page.

I was eventually reintroduced to his demanding spirit when asked by Goldwater to visit Phoenix in order to take part in a money-raising event for the benefit of Jon Kyl. The evening event was carefully planned, and the organizers clearly anticipated the presence of the Republican mandarinate of Arizona. I was the principal speaker, and George Will had been induced to come to the scene for the formal purpose of introducing me to the seven hundred–odd guests, for the informal purpose of introducing to that part of the world his glowing presence as a leading theologian-in-waiting for the conservative movement.

We met at the hotel and were advised that the senator was not feeling strong enough and had been forbidden by his new wife, Susan, to participate formally in the scheduled events. He agreed to stay home that evening, but insisted on a private meeting at his house with George Will and me.

I found him in many ways unchanged from the Goldwater of thirty years before, though manifestly less inclined to hand-to-hand combat with dissenters. At the last minute, late in the afternoon, he made a move to attend the dinner, and went so far as jauntily to command Lazaro to bring him his black tie. Confronted with this mutinous challenge, Susan soon assembled all her authority as parietal mistress of Be-Nun-I-Kin.

What Goldwater did get away with was an appearance the next day at a small gathering of twenty or thirty of the faithful at a garden in the folds of the Ritz-Carlton Hotel. And there we all were witness to an absolute revival. Goldwater led off by introducing me, who had been charged with generating enthusiasm for Jon Kyl's campaign for the Senate. I had experienced Goldwater's effusiveness in the past but never on quite the order of that afternoon. If I had been White House chief of staff, chief justice of the Supreme Court, and the author of *Progress and Poverty*, he could not have gone further in stressing my eminence to the potential philanthropists, or in elaborating on his appreciation of me and my work.

Returning to our hotel rooms, I blurted out to George Will, whom I had known since the early seventies, that our hero Goldwater was losing hold of essential measurements in social and political history. Nothing surprises George Will, so he was able to respond cheerfully that that was the way Goldwater works and I should forget about it.

I both did and did not. I easily slept through the night without being distracted by his hagiographic account of my career, but I did not shake off the intensity of the experience of finding myself in the company of the old Goldwater, who had defied American taboos by running for president without compromising his principles and who, however momentarily, had arrested the attention of twenty-seven million voters who thought him unique in American history.

And that was that. No one else comes to mind who sustained for so long a comparable reputation for candor and courage. Over the years, if active in the political community, one comes across rejected aspirants for the presidency. But even in that rare company Goldwater, whether initiating a call from the South Pole to my wife, or puddle-jumping the Grand Canyon for his friends, was unique, and will forever remain so.

ACKNOWLEDGMENTS

I was not planning to write a book on Barry Goldwater, but when it was suggested that I do so, I had one of those buoyancies ("Mr. Eiffel, why don't you build a tower?"). This was easily accounted for. I knew Senator Goldwater, had shared time and experiences with him, was a partisan in his bloody political campaign, and several times visited him at his home. I wish he had lived to read this book, while agreeing that it is always safer to write about friends after they are dead.

I leap quickly to acknowledge the Goldwater Institute in Phoenix, where I was placed in the hands of Arwynn Mattix. Her helpfulness is impossible to overstate. I will say simply that this book could not have been done without her. She is a storehouse of Goldwater information—piles and books and libraries of it, I have to imagine—that supply the researcher with as much raw material as he could legitimately want, or hope to have access to. I am indebted also to Barry

Goldwater Jr., who helped me in several ways, his friendship opening many doors.

I have most ardently to acknowledge Anthony Dick, who was at my side during the composition of the book. After graduating from the University of Virginia, he spent a year honing his editorial skills at *National Review*, the fortnightly journal of opinion with which I have been associated pre partum, in partu, and post partum. He resolved to go on to law school—which he is now doing, at Stanford—but I persuaded him to hold off until he had served as my research assistant and right hand in the writing of this book. He was with me through the whole of the period I devoted to the project in Bermuda last spring. It is a haunting memory that we worked in a huge, exquisite seaside mansion, suddenly made available to my wife and me. But her illness proved too serious for her to travel (she died the following month), and although we continued to expect her arrival, she never came. So it was just the beautiful villa in its handsome setting, the discriminating owner's library of several hundred movies on DVD, a fine cook—and, of course, Goldwater.

I cannot add much to the tributes I have already paid to my editorial quartet, who have helped me for so many years on so many projects. Lois Wallace is my agent and superintends most of my professional life. Samuel Vaughan remains my editor par excellence. In my office I have for many years relied on Frances Bronson, as I still do. Linda Bridges is my in-house editor and researcher and dear and competent friend and mood regulator. Again, I thank them all, as I do also William Frucht, vice president of Basic Books, who came up with the idea for this book.

And, finally, Barry Goldwater, who animates these pages even as he did a listless political party a half century ago.

—WFB
Stamford, Connecticut
November 2007

INDEX

Basic Ideas

Every great idea—whether embodied in a speech, a mathematical equation, a song, or a work of art—has an origin, a birth, and a life of enduring influence. In each book in the Basic Ideas series, a leading authority offers a concise biography of a text that transformed its world, and ours.